Harry Williams

An Australian Golfing Tragedy

by
June Senyard

Ryan Publishing

First published 1998 by Ryan Publishing
24/20 Commercial Road
(P.O. Box 7680)
Melbourne, Victoria, Australia, 3004
Ph : 61 3 9820 0988   Fax: 61 3 9866 5387
Email : books@ryanpub.com.au
Website : www.ryanpub.com.au

National Library of Australia Cataloguing-in-Publication entry

Senyard, June.
   Harry Williams - An Australian Golfing Tragedy

ISBN: 1 876498 01 3

1. Williams, Harry, 1915-1961. 2. Golfers - Australia - Biography.
I. Title

796.352092

Contents

Harry Williams - Career Record

1931   Australian Amateur Championship
Victorian Amateur Championship
Victorian Amateur Foursome Championship (with R. Harris)

1932   *Australasian* Foursome Shield (with A.W. Jackson)

1933   Victoria Golf Club Championship

1934   Victorian Amateur Championship
Victoria Golf Club Championship

1935   Victorian Amateur Championship
Victorian Amateur Foursome Championship (with H.R. Payne)

1936   Australian Open Championship: Runner-up and Leading Amateur
Victorian Amateur Championship
Australian Amateur Foursome Championship (with H.R. Payne)
Australasian Foursome Shield (with H.R. Payne)
Victoria Golf Club Championship

1937   Australian Amateur Championship

1939   Victorian Amateur Championship
Victorian Amateur Foursome Championship (with A.V. Rae)
Australasian Foursome Shield (with H.R. Payne)
Victoria Golf Club Championship

1940   Phillipines Open Championship: Leading Amateur

Acknowledgements

Just as there were many people who admired Harry Williams in the 1930s, so there has been much support to tell his story to a different generation sixty years later. It says a great deal for golf as a sport and even as a way of life that older golfers are in such good shape and have so much to contribute.

To my publisher Graeme Ryan who initiated the project and cheerfully embarked on a range of activities to ensure its successful completion. To Sonia Jennings who undertook research on Harry with great enthusiasm and, in pursuit of the illusory past, showed the keen eye of the best detective for detail, good counsel on the twists and turns of the investigation and a willingness to embark on various adventures along the way.

To Eileen Grigg who generously shared memories of her cousin Harry so that he emerged as a friend as well as a golfer.

To Darryl Cox, Max Eise, Clive Glasson and Norman Von Nida who willingly shared their knowledge of Harry Williams the golfer.

To Alf (Okey) King Snr, Dorothy Collins and Ray Jones who expanded the horizons of the investigation by recounting stories of Melbourne in the past, of bookies on and off the course, betting and nightlife.

To Clive Glasson at the Victoria Golf Club, Michael Tinsley at the Public Records Office, Tom Duguid at the Australian Golf Union, Peter Coster at the Herald Sun and Margaret Paul who provided access to important sources. To Nigel Ford who explained the intricacies of various legal documents and Anne Hider who provided background to city dining.

To David Studham and Ross Peacock at the MCG Library who administer a valuable resource for any sporting research. To Rob Vanderzalm, who wrote the first article and to Elaine, John and Anthony who made helpful comments along the way.

1

Former Star Golfer Found Dead In Flat. The evening issue of the *Herald* on 14 December 1961 caught the story. In the morning, the *Age* carried the news with the headline, Ex-Amateur Golf Champion Found Dead and the *Sun News Pictorial* completed reporting on the event with Tragedy Of A Golfing Wonder Boy accompanied by a photograph of Harry Williams completing a full golf swing.

The police had been called to a flat in Hartwood Street, East Kew late in the afternoon of Wednesday December 13 following a neighbour's call that there was a strong smell of gas. On entering, First Constable MacRae found the bodies of Harry Williams, his mother Emma Madge, and their Australian terrier lying on the floor in the kitchen, all dead. Strips of feltex had been stuffed into gaps between the doors and the floor and a note was on the kitchen bench. There was a lettuce and some butter in the refrigerator and in the other rooms of the flat, there were three crates of belongings still unpacked

To the 1961 reader, with the newspapers full of the forthcoming Federal elections, the headlines on the back page merely marked the passing of some sporting personality from the time before the war. The manner of death was sensational but it created only a fleeting interest.

Nevertheless, the story was news to a circle of people who had played golf in the 1930s or who were generally interested in golf in Australia. For Harry Williams, during the 1930s, had been a major star of the Australian sporting world and now, news of his death revived those memories.

At the funeral on the Monday at the chapel of Drayton and Garsen's in Glen Iris, a small crowd assembled. The mourners broke up into several groups. There were the relatives and neighbours from South Yarra and Canterbury, there were a few mates from Harry's places of work and there were men who had played golf with Harry. They were there as a tribute to the memory of Harry as a golfer they had watched with pleasure. They were also indulging a sense of nostalgia for a time when golf seemed always to be played on wonderful clear crisp days with men full of good humour and good-fellowship.

It was a hot day and as one of Harry's golfing acquaintances was heard to remark, *he was sure Harry would have liked a good cold ale under such conditions*. After the formalities of the cremation at Springvale, Harry's golfing friends repaired to drink to Harry's life. None of them had seen Harry that recently, indeed some hadn't seen him for several years. At first the talk was about the events surrounding Harry's death, filling in the details of when and where it had happened.

You'd wonder what was so bad that made them decide to commit suicide?

I was talking to someone outside the chapel and he said that they had been talking to Harry and Doll a couple of days ago and they had sounded fine.

But it must have been planned. They say that the note was quite clear, they didn't have any money left and no hope of making any.

I think Harry had been put off - part of the recession I suppose. Not that he ever was in a permanent job. I don't think he was cut out for work. Remember he had that hernia - and then during the war, he had asthma and was discharged. He was never what you'd call a strapping young bloke was he?

They must have run out of the money Eric left to them.

That was a fair bit of money, wasn't it? At the time, people talked of it as quite a fortune.

2

They'd only been in the flat six weeks and already were behind in their rent so that sounds as if they were in a bad way. No, they must have decided that there was no future.

At this, the men fell silent for they were remembering very clearly how, at one time, if anyone had said that of Harry Williams the statement would have been met with disbelief. When the conversation resumed, the men had moved on to the real enigma for them, the rise and rise of Harry Williams and then a decline into oblivion. When Harry had chosen to relinquish his place at the top of Australian golf over twenty years before, they had been baffled. Now, with the bizarre ending of suicide, the debate was rekindled. They fell to talking about Harry's brilliance.

For someone who was so long and gangly, his timing was very precise. He could really hit the golf ball. I was playing with him one day at Victoria and I remember him hitting the green at the 11th - it's a par four - with a one iron from the tee. That was 405 yards. I've never seen anyone do that at Victoria since then.

Yes, he was a prodigious hitter. I remember on Sunday morning - it was a pennant practice match and he drove this 2-iron, three hundred yards or more. And just completely casual about it.

I think the best shot I ever saw played by anyone was one of Harry's. It was at the 16th hole at Commonwealth – the dog-leg hole around the lake there, 408 yards it was then. Harry hadn't had a good drive and so he probably still was at least 230 yards to the green over the lake. He hit a one-iron to within 18 inches of the flag and ended up with a birdie three.

He had the smoothest swing I've ever seen.

Yes, and he was so accurate. He could land a ball within a yard of the pin from any direction. He was playing at Royal Melbourne one day and drove the green of the par 4 10th West, fading the ball in beautifully. I forget who he was playing with, but they bet him to do it again. He did. Then they said that it was because the shape of *the hole favoured a left-hander's fade. So he got out two more balls and hit them on to the green by drawing the ball out over the trees on the left. Yes, he could do anything with a golf ball.*

He'd be the best Australian left-hander ever.

I'd say he was the best left or right handed.

Of course, he was brilliant but he was always a bit off-hand wasn't he? He had a big reputation as combining golf and gambling.

They laughed.

Did any of his horses come home?

No, I don't think so. Harry was never particularly lucky when it came to gambling. But he could certainly win on the golf course.

The men began to argue over Harry's triumphs; how many Victorian titles, how many Australian titles, how many championships at Victoria Golf Club he had won. In the process, they cast their minds back to the events that shaped the golfing world then. They remembered the names of the other golfers who were playing at the time of Harry's triumphs - Ivo Whitton the legendary Royal Melbourne amateur, Mick Ryan, the ex-South Melbourne footballer turned golfer, Jim Ferrier from Sydney who was now in the United States, Norman Von Nida prominent on the world stage and the golfers who visited Australia over the period - Walter Hagen, Gene Sarazen and Bobby Locke. Names that enchanted the golfing public and Harry Williams had been one of them. But he had turned his back on this golden stage and around this decision, there developed as many explanations as golf balls on a practice tee.

Of course, it was Doll - he could never get away from her. Remember how she used to go to all the tournaments, was always running after him. A mummy's boy. She wouldn't let him out of Australia. She certainly scared the girls off. Anyone who talked to Harry knew they would have to run the gauntlet with Doll. But then Doll always treated him like a child, waited on him hand and foot.

4

I don't know. Harry didn't let that stop him having a good life. Back there, at the 1937 Championships, I think, I was talking to her after the round, and she said, she was worried sick about Harry, how he was out to all hours, how she never knew where he was or what he was doing.

Doll always said that he got into bad company. But she used to like a good time too so I don't suppose Harry took much notice of her. She and my mother were great friends, they used to be together in the gallery and she said that Doll was worried that Harry had some internal sickness.

Oh, no, I don't think it was his health particularly. I think it was more deep-seated than that. I think it was more his father. Harry told me once about how his father used to belt him when he was a kid. Harry was always good company but I reckon his father belted the confidence out of him.

Thoroughly immersed in their theories of human behaviour and the tragic irony of Harry's death, the talk came to rest on just how good Harry had been as a golfer. The men began to debate the relative merits of the major players of the decade who had played with Harry. All had recognised his brilliance. Before long they were back to the old question that haunted every discussion of Harry Williams, why had he let such talent dissipate to finish by dying in a gas-filled kitchen in East Kew? Even as the men made their way to their cars, they were still arguing.

2

Henry Llewellyn Carlington Williams was born on 12 July 1915. Harry's names marked his patrimony: Henry and Llewellyn for his paternal grandfather and Carlington for his maternal grandfather. They were names of men who were successful nineteenth century immigrants and had established themselves as part of Melbourne's prosperous middle class.

Harry's father, Eric was born in 1893 and grew up in Brunswick. His father was Henry Harold Llewellyn Williams but he was known as Harry Williams. More important for Harry Williams than the clothes which he packed to take to the Australian colonies, was the knowledge he carried of his Welsh experience in working with iron and steel. Harry Williams was a drop-forger, working hot pieces of metal placed between dies by the blows of a drop hammer. When Harry Williams established a foundry in Weston Street, Brunswick, he was part of the network of small industrial sites that fuelled the huge expansion of Melbourne during the late nineteenth century.

Operating a small business, Harry and Mary Williams carried weight in the local community. They lived at 'Nalang', 69 Park Street, a sought after area in the locality, for it fronted the open spaces of Royal Park. The view from the front parlour, however, was heavily shrouded by layers of lace and velvet curtains and the mantlepiece, piano and sideboards, loaded with figurines, photographs and knick knacks encouraged the owners to take pride more in this display of their own success than of the immediate vista.

There were two children, Eric and Thelma. Thelma, it was expected, would marry and devote her life to husband and family. Eric, on the other hand, required an occupation. A period in the foundry earned him the right to call himself, Engineer, but he had little interest in the business, preferring the picture of himself in a suit and tie in a less grubby environment.

When Eric began to court Emma Halfey, he was able to convince his father that she wanted a husband with clean hands. Eric left the foundry behind him. Eric's engagement to Emma Madge Dagmar Halfey was most pleasing to the Williams family. Through the intricate maxims of social precedence of Edwardian Melbourne, Emma Madge Dagmar Halfey was a good catch. Her parents may have failed the test if they stood alone but the heights to which Emma's grandfather had reached more than balanced this dip in the family fortunes. For Emma was the granddaughter of John Halfey, a nineteenth century immigrant to Victoria who, through his life story, exemplified all the hallmarks of the successful adventurer.

John Halfey at the age of 26, left England to escape a marriage he had come to regret. The son of a boarding house keeper, Halfey had taken up with a servant girl and in 1849 eloped with her to Gretna Green where they were married. Within eighteen months, however, he left her and their baby daughter and, under the name of his brother-in-law, sailed for the Victorian goldfields.

Once in the colony, Halfey made for the Bendigo goldfields and in the alluvial soil of the Sandhurst flats found the gold that was to set him up for life. By 1855, he was back in Melbourne and with the capital won on the goldfields looked to invest in the expanding economy. Halfey also looked to re-establishing a family. He began to pay court to Annie Lane, daughter of a master mariner. From 1858, negotiating a marriage settlement with Annie as well as extricating himself from the legal complexities surrounding his first marriage occupied Halfey. He and Annie were finally married in February 1863.

John Halfey became a prominent figure in 'Marvellous' Melbourne as it was often called. He remained enthusiastic about the colony, investing in shares in mines at Bendigo and Walhalla and the river trade on the Murray River. As well, he moved into city property, banking and insurance and took up the role of Director in a range of major companies. Some of Halfey's business interests were more entrepreneurial. In a city where Melba began her singing career in 1884 and where premieres of Gilbert and Sullivan played to packed houses, shares in the Opera-house Company combined fashion and speculation for Halfey. Similarly, Halfey invested in the Bay Excursion Company, hoping to benefit from the thousands of suburban families who, with the privilege of a weekend, thronged the beaches in summer.

Wealth assumed rank and John Halfey was not opposed to suggestions that his success should have a public face. At first he directed his interests to Kew, serving on the Kew Municipal Council, acting as a trustee of the first Holy Trinity Church of England and presiding as a magistrate in the Court of Petty Sessions. These were stepping-stones to a seat in parliament. In 1864, Halfey stood as representative for Sandhurst in the Legislative Assembly and was elected. His performance in the House, however, did not satisfy his electorate and in 1868, when the elections came around again, Halfey was soundly beaten. Each of his subsequent attempts to return to parliament - in 1870, 1871 and 1888 - were unsuccessful.

By this time, though, Halfey enjoyed considerable influence in the city. From 1871, Halfey was part of a syndicate that purchased the Melbourne Newspaper Co Ltd - he and S W Winter, being the major investors. Thereafter Halfey managed the *Herald* and conducted his affairs from the office at the eastern end of Little Collins Street. In 1872, he was appointed official assignee of insolvent estates, official liquidator and commissioner of the Supreme Court.

John and Annie Halfey were amongst the most prominent residents of the salubrious suburb of Kew. They established themselves at 'Ordsall', a Renaissance style mansion, on the corner of Cotham Road and Charles Street with a holiday home at Sorrento. John and Annie Halfey produced a family of three sons and two daughters, of whom Frank, their eldest son drowned in the Yarra River when he was ten and Violet died in infancy.

In January 1889, John Halfey died suddenly. He left an estate of over £190,000, a fortune that ensured his family could sustain an affluent lifestyle. John Halfey was buried in the Borondoora Cemetery, laid out in 1861, when he had been most active on the Kew Municipal Council. Planted with conifers and cypresses, the cemetery offered a suitable site for residents to take a contemplative stroll. Now, the monument of John Halfey, with its uppermost angel, often referred to as the Herald angel, presided over all.

Meanwhile, the family went its different ways. John Percival Frederick or as he was known, Percy, the youngest, had married Emma Marston the preceding year, 1888. Emma's father, Carlington G. E. Marston was a pharmacist at 178 Smith Street, Collingwood but, like the Halfeys, sought the more commodious mansions of Kew for his family's residence. The Marstons lived at 'Wimba', Cotham Road, Kew. In quick succession, Emma gave birth to a daughter, known as Popsie, a son - John Percival Carlington - and on 17 February 1893, twins, Emma Madge and Edith Mary. So pleased were the parents on the arrival of twins that they immediately became Doll - she looked just like a doll,and Queenie - she just held herself so.

After John Halfey's death, Annie Halfey left for England with her second son, leaving Percy and Emma at 'Ordsall'. Percy and Emma proved unsatisfactory tenants and were evicted from 'Ordsall' when Doll and

Queenie were only little. An alcoholic, Percy died in 1902 leaving Emma, now quite unfit, to bring up the children. As a result, John Percival was packed off to Scotch College and the girls to Vaucluse in Richmond.

A convent life, it was thought, would surely deter the girls from following in the steps of their unfortunate mother. Certainly, every minute of their lives was organised and supervised so there was no time for attempting the sinful while morning and evening prayers were absolutely obligatory. Generally, they remembered the main event of the day as dinner. Under the vigilant eye of the nun on duty, Queenie and Doll learned the importance of table manners and of the etiquette of demure and restrained eating habits.

Doll and Queenie were always best friends but sometimes Doll could try even her sister's patience. Each month, the girls were allowed a visit to the city, to pick up their allowance from the family law firm, signing the book as they did so. One month, when Queenie arrived to collect her allowance, the clerk pointed to the book, saying:
Now, you know you can't collect your allowance twice over.
Queenie looked at the signature and recognised Doll's handwriting. When she remonstrated with her, Doll argued that she had needed the money to buy a pair of shoes she'd seen and, shrugging her shoulders, added Anyway, you have plenty of money.
Queenie didn't agree, That's because I look after my allowance and don't spend it all on the day I get it.

By the time, Queenie and Doll left school, the family home was at 'Brayton', Canterbury road, St Kilda and the girls came out in the last years of Edwardian Melbourne. There was their brother, John, and Queenie and Doll. Their oldest sister married and moved away from the family altogether. The twins had to take responsibility in the home, for their mother was generally indisposed.

Canterbury Road was one of the main avenues linking St Kilda and the city. It ran parallel to Beaconsfield Parade, which had been built as a military road against a possible Russian invasion and in 1887 opened in commemoration of Queen Victoria's jubilee. Suburban housing filled the space between. After the Depression of the 1890s, the new houses built in the open spaces were much smaller with reduced frontages, leaving Canterbury Road and Beaconsfield Parade as corridors of substantial residences. The electric train ran along the east side.

By this time, St Kilda had two distinct domains, the wide residential streets of respectable suburban homes and the foreshore along the beach, a destination for all of Melbourne on summer evenings and weekends. With the construction of St Kilda pier and the opening of Luna Park in 1907 and the Palais de Danse in 1908, the entertainments there overshadowed the more staid arrangements of the local residents based around tennis parties and church. The new 'mixed bathing' was an issue and municipal notices required neck to knee bathers. Queenie and Doll, mindful of their complexions, under broad brimmed hats strolled along the pier or licked ice-creams and watched the different entertainers who appeared in the gardens of the Esplanade in summer. They did not venture to upset the conventional notions of feminine modesty by attempting more than a discreet paddle in the shallows.

Despite the routine of domestic chores, Queenie and Doll also enjoyed a social round of visits and events. They were both considered to be pretty although Doll thought that their shortsightedness, which required glasses, was a definite problem. But the girls were popular and there were always invitations to parties and dances. Going out was often a lengthy process because Doll would always try on different hats or scarves or gloves and parade up and down the room for Queenie to pronounce upon. Finally, Queenie would cut the performance short by saying, Come on, you look lovely and bustle Doll out the door.

While hansom cabs and all types of horse-drawn vehicles crowded the thoroughfares, Queenie and Doll now had the option of the electric railway to take them into the city at any time. Whenever possible, Doll urged Queenie to take a cable tram into the city, especially to Do the Block in Collins Street if they were still there of a late afternoon. The shop windows, displaying the latest from London, the busy cafes and the passing parade of people made Doll skip with pleasure.

Although their own parents were regarded as black sheep within the family, Queenie and Doll enjoyed the satisfaction that they could point to concrete evidence of both their grandfathers' part in the bustling life of the metropolis. A trip on the cable tram up past the Eastern Hill Fire Station and the Cyclorama and around through the large furniture stores of Gertrude and Smith Streets also carried them past Grandpa Marston's pharmacy. Then, there were constant reminders of grandpa Halfey throughout the city - the offices of the Herald, the imposing buildings that housed the companies of which he had been Director - and the houses at Kew and Sorrento. Such obvious reminders of an important past impressed the girls and the social circle in which they moved.

With grandparents who had made a successful transition from England to the colonies, Queenie and Doll were encouraged to believe that all that was good emanated from England. The throne and the Empire were unquestioned certainties of their world. While the dust swirled up Canterbury Road in summer and the winter gales roared in from the Bay, they yearned for a white Christmas and for the song of the nightingale. They eagerly consulted the newspapers for news of all that was fashionable and the latest in England and the scandals surrounding Edward VIII were devoured as the lifestyle of the rich and famous.

With this apprenticeship, the twins were eager to embark on marriage. From their various suitors, the girls readily secured husbands and planned a double wedding at Holy Trinity, St Kilda. Each brought their own substantial legacies to their marriages. In 1914, at the age of twenty-one, Queenie married Harold Lake, an engineer in the Post Master General's Department and Doll married Eric Llewellyn Williams, who was also termed an engineer. To Doll, Eric was tall and handsome. He was about six feet and quite rugged so that with Doll on his arm, they made a good-looking couple. Australia may have been at war but the two young couples standing on the steps of the church considered their futures to be assured.

3

On 12 July 1915, when Henry Llewellyn Carlington Williams was born, the young Australian male was winning recognition on the world stage. Harry's birth came in the lull between the storming of the cliffs and the Turkish counterattack at Gallipoli of late April and May and the Suvla Bay landing in August. For Harry, each year, the solemn celebration of Anzac would reinforce the message of the sacrifice that took place in these months. But also of importance was the elaboration of the heroic figure of the Anzac as a model of the typical Australian for succeeding generations. Baby Harry Williams could confidently expect to be recognised as Australian in any international forum but whether he would be seen as a typical Australian was more of an open question.

In Melbourne, in the winter of 1915, Doll, was learning the tasks of motherhood. In August, Queenie gave birth to Eileen Dagmar and together, the two young matrons conferred on the progress of their babies. Meanwhile, the war ground on, the early enthusiasms overlaid by the pressures of the war effort, by grieving and by division. A heavy blanket descended as moral reformers, stimulated by demands for austerity, resumed their battles to further curtail drinking and gambling and the conscription referenda was bitterly fought out around the nation. Yet, in the private world of Doll and Queenie, there was optimism. In 1918, Marie Jean was born to Harold and Queenie and in 1919, Joan Dagmar to Eric and Doll. The family circles were now complete.

Like the card game of Happy Families, the Williams family of Eric the Father, Doll the Mother, Young Harry and Little Joan viewed the 1920s with optimism. It appeared to those who enjoyed a comfortable income that the pleasures of modern life spread before them enhanced by the comfort and efficiency of technology. The rate of home building in metropolitan Melbourne increased dramatically. House allotments, with a minimum of fifty feet frontage and strict health regulations that required separate kitchen and bathroom plumbing and access to light and air for every room, were laid out across the flat land stretching from St Kilda to Brighton, often subdivisions of large properties. The villages, of Sandringham, Mentone and Hampton were absorbed by the urban expansion to the southeast of the city. With Port Phillip Bay giving the area definition to the west, the Lake's and the Williams's made their homes in this heartland of twentieth century Melbourne suburbia.

Although the lives of Queenie and Doll had run parallel up to the end of World War I, they now began to diverge slightly but significantly. Queenie and Harold Lake built a Californian bungalow in Head Street, Elwood and there settled into the routines of suburban life. It was a good position, there was an open park area opposite and the beach beckoned at the end of the street. Harold, in his work in the Post Master General's Department had a secure job and brought home a good salary. Every morning he left for his office in the impressive General Post Office on the corner of Bourke and Elizabeth Streets in the city. Both Queenie and Doll only learned to cook and to run a home on getting married. Although Queenie never enjoyed particularly good health, she became a good housekeeper and an excellent cook.

Meanwhile, Eric and Doll occupied a succession of houses in the streets to the south in Brighton, the height of social status in Melbourne's southeast. At first, Eric and Doll leased 35 Martin Street, gracing the house with the name, 'Dagmar' after Doll's family. Then there were houses in Drake Street, St Kilda Street, Wellington Street, St George's Court and Birdswood Avenue. No longer regarded just as a seaside resort, but a fashionable suburb, Brighton was a solid area of substantial houses from the nineteenth century and newer bungalows, filling in the

15

vacant allotments. It was a society based on the private domains of the quarter acre block. There was only a handful of hotels. In 1920, when a ballot on drinking regulations was held throughout the metropolitan area, the people of Brighton voted for even tighter controls. It was also a suburb with some pretensions to gentility, possessing numbers of well-established professional and merchant families prepared to organise and maintain educational, sporting and cultural bodies.

Eric considered various options for his future and for his family's livelihood. After the war, Eric, who had not enlisted because of his young family and his work in manufacturing, found that returned men were often given preference. Although Eric continued to state his occupation as engineer, he looked to more managerial positions. At one stage, Eric and Doll leased a large old house in Wellington Street that they proposed to run as a guesthouse. This, they thought, would combine Eric's skills as manager and Doll's charms as hostess. They hired the necessary staff and advertised their establishment as suitable for the social set, dressing for dinner a requisite. However, the demands of such a business were too much and they soon retired from it.

The Williams's were prosperous and they were able to embrace much of post-war life that was new and exciting. Most people in Melbourne at the time either took the tram or the train or they walked. The Williams's and the Lake's rode in cars. To Eric and Doll, a motorcar conjured up power and status. Just the names - Hupmobile, Oldsmobile, Chevrolet, Packard - promised the delight of motoring. The main boulevards leading into the city - St Kilda Road, Beaconsfield Parade, Victoria Parade, Royal Parade - took on new meaning as the motor car proceeded in lordly fashion to take precedence over the horse-drawn vehicles and the bicycles. To step onto the running board, to squeeze the horn, Eric and Doll were at their happiest when they were behind the steering wheel. Both Doll and Queenie drove, their expectations of benefiting from modern technology untroubled by conventions that this may be for males only.

In the home, Doll, like Queenie, learned to be a housekeeper and cook. At the Lake's and at the Williams's households, a series of servants lived in to maintain the daily routines of the laundry, kitchen, nursery and of the home generally. There was the new labour saving device of the vacuum cleaner and the telephone to make life easier but there was still much to do. Doll became an excellent cook and was very particular about her furniture and the décor of the rooms. Over the years the fairly constant changing of addresses gave her the opportunity to try out many different schemes and arrangements.

Harry's earliest memories of his mother were the scent of her powder and the smooth feel of silk stockings and the bows on her shoes. When Doll was out, she was great company. There were invitations to afternoon tea, bridge afternoons, shopping expeditions, parties and shows and the races. Usually, Doll escaped to her sister's at least once a week to sit and gossip about the children and the doings of the family and Queenie laughed appreciatively at her descriptions of people and events. Then, other relatives and friends would often come over and the afternoon and evening would pass quickly in eddies of laughter and conversation. Doll was vivacious and lively and at cards or dancing or dining enjoyed the sociability of any occasion. To Harry, paraded in his pyjamas before his parents to say goodnight, they appeared, dressed in their best and ready for an evening out or getting ready to entertain at home, to be absolutely splendid.

As he left the chubbiness of the toddler behind him, Tunny, the family's pet name for Harry, took more after the Williams side of the family. He was tall for his age and dressed in short trousers and shirts he often seemed all knees and legs. He learned to occupy himself as he was usually sent out into the back yard to play while Doll attended to baby Joan or Pat as the family often called her. For Harry, there was always the family dog for company or whipping his top along the path but he spent hours playing with his collection of marbles, rolling them along the path, making them jump, admiring their brilliant colours and polishing his prize bulls-eyes.

When Harry and Eileen were five, Doll and Queenie discussed how to induct their older children into the demands of schooling. They selected the Miss Macauley's school in Murphy Street near the corner of North Road, Gardenvale as suitable guides to Harry and Eileen's first steps in learning. The kindergarten was close so they could walk there. For Harry and Eileen, it was a happy time. There were only about fifty children there and the mixture of play and learning was conducted in a relaxed and sympathetic style by Miss Daisy and her sister.

Harry began to take an interest in the wider world. It was the aeroplane that appeared to Harry the most extraordinary. From when he was five, Harry was kept abreast of the famous aviators from the illustrations in the newspapers. He learned to identify Ross and Charles Kingsford Smith. Then there was Parer and McIntosh who cut down the trip from England to Australia to ninety days. Bert Hinkler. Amy Johnson. Each flight was another cut in time between Melbourne and the rest of the world and Harry followed the leaps across the map on the front pages of the Sun News Pictorial. Here were heroes. Some were British, some were American, but some were also Australian. To Harry, the glamour of aviation also carried the fear of failure. In 1922, Sir Ross as he was by then, disappeared. Harry carried the hope that he would be found but secretly knew that this could not be.

But there were also dramatic moments in Harry's own life. There were occasional visits to great-uncle Harry Marston, who lived in a flat in Glenferrie Road. Great-uncle Harry was a shadowy figure who sat and talked with Doll and Queenie. It was his valet who intimidated the children. He would ceremoniously set up a little table with fruit knife and plates for each of them watching over them as they nervously exercised their manners. Sometimes, Harry was taken to visit his grandmother Williams who rather scared him by examining him closely from top to toe when they arrived and asked him difficult questions to which he was expected to reply correctly.

One day, Doll and Queenie packed the children into the car and set out for a long trip to the country. It seemed to Harry that they travelled for hours and hours and then when they reached their destination, the children were left in the car while Doll and Queenie disappeared behind high walls. When they came out Doll and Queenie told them they had been to visit their grandmother. The children were rather surprised as they had not even known they had a grandmother. She was now living out her days in the care of the State at Beechworth. It was a family secret that remained so.

At home, Harry only gradually became aware of his sister Joan as a possible playmate. As she stumbled into his games and then tried out her first words and gradually asserted herself, he treated her indulgently. If she interrupted too much, he called Doll. When Harry was seven and Joan nearly four, however, the two children had been playing in the garden. Joan complained that she was hot and had a headache. Doll thought it was just tiredness and sat her up for tea. Joan was quiet and pushed her boiled egg away saying she wasn't hungry. When Doll felt her forehead, it was clammy and she put her straight into bed.

Once in bed, Joan did not fall into a healthy sleep but began to whimper that she was hot, that she had a stomach ache, that she wanted to be sick, and her neck was sore. Doll lay with her and rocked her until she slept fitfully. But later, on going in to check Joan again, Doll was frightened to find her in a high fever, her nightgown and bedclothes wet through, her eyes glittering and her body shivering. She yelled for Eric to go for the doctor. Harry, awakened by the lights and his father's departure, tiptoed into where Doll held Joan. What's wrong with Pat? he asked apprehensively. Doll turned to him, her distressed face telling him that something terrible was happening. He clung to her and stroked Joan's head.

When the doctor walked in with Eric, he was not reassuring. He asked Doll how long Joan had been sick and shook his head, grim-faced. It was not influenza. It was meningitis and he prepared them for the worst, for the fatality rate was high, up to 70%. Joan did not regain consciousness. She died, a day short of her fourth birthday. In death, as quiet and stillness overtook her body, Joan appeared to Doll more beautiful than she had ever known her. But it was a very sombre reflection.

All Doll's attention now centred on Harry. The sudden onset of Joan's illness haunted her. It had been so random and she racked her mind for how she may have avoided the tragedy. She watched Harry with an eagle eye for colds or sniffles that might develop into something worse and chased after him with coats and caps to protect him from the winter cold. Harry, however, defied all such threats, remained robust and continued to add further inches to his height.

Harry learned to be a good boy. Although Harry, now an only child, may have been considered to be spoilt, Doll was very particular about politeness. Harry addressed Queenie and Harold by their first names but in their own street, he called all the neighbours, Mr or Mrs or Miss. When he was down to the corner store with a message for two eggs or a shillings worth of biscuits, it was Mr Jones and when the plumber came to fix the leaking tap, he would greet him politely, *Good morning, Mr Kelly*. As Doll explained, politeness was the difference between the desirable state of being well behaved and the unhappy condition of the vulgar.

Manners, too, were essential. Within the home, Harry's father, Eric might be unrestrained but, out on the street, he was gallant. Never without a hat, Eric would raise it for any of their female neighbours and would always walk on the gutter side, expecting to repulse any dastardly attack on the women he escorted. Then there was the matter of noise. For a woman to be shrill or a man to yell out or whistle in public betrayed them as lower class and forfeited them a place in polite society. Harry learned too that men could utter a discreet *bugger* or *bloody* when telling a story if it was all males together but, in mixed company, jokes and comment had to be censored in view of the ladies present.

On the Sabbath the Williams family rested. Sundays settled as a curtain of boredom on suburban Melbourne. There was no sport, no newspapers, no theatre and no films. The sound of the church bells and the exodus of families from their streets at the hour for morning service left others attending to the lawn mowing and cooking the Sunday roast. The early Anglicanism of the Halfey's and the Welsh non-conformism of the Williams's had ebbed. Certainly, Doll and Eric were not backsliders. Weddings, baptisms and funerals all required a church setting and, if necessary, special occasions such as a celebratory service might be observed. But, generally, Sunday was a day for a substantial meal and then a drive in the country or down to Frankston that fitted within the limits set by the restrictions on Sunday entertainment and its strict observance as *a day of rest*.

All domestic arrangements were eclipsed late in 1923, when Thelma, Eric's sister, announced plans for her wedding at St Paul's Cathedral and asked Harry and Eileen to be trainbearers. The children, listening to Queenie and Doll, knew it was a special event for it occupied a great deal of their conversations. There were fittings and rehearsals and then the day itself.

It was a 6 p.m. wedding and Thelma, on the arm of her father walked into St Paul's preceded by sixteen choir boys. Thelma's long dress of ivory velvet brocade was swathed across the front in Egyptian fashion and a long silver train draped from one shoulder. This was in charge of Harry and Eileen; Harry, a little gentleman in cream gabardine suit with short trousers and long socks and Eileen, captivating in a short petal frock of cream and mauve georgette with poke bonnet. The bridesmaids in silver tissue hats and dresses of lavender and jade green georgette embossed with silver completed the bridal group.

The champagne dinner for one hundred and twenty guests at 9 Darling Street was followed by a dance. For the reception, Thelma changed into an evening frock of pale blue satin lumineaux with a blue satin wrap embossed with gold and a high roll collar of blue chiffon velvet and on her head, a diamente headdress. Eric and Thelma's mother was also very smart in a black chiffon velvet gown with panel and cabachon of jet with a small black hat trimmed with a quill. The honeymoon was spent at Mt Buffalo. Long after the wedding, the bridegroom's gift of a bracelet for Eileen and a monogrammed hairbrush for Harry, together with the studio photographs of the wedding, remained as tangible reminders of a momentous social occasion.

4

By the time of Thelma's wedding, Harry had already turned eight and Eric and Doll looked for a suitable school for him. Harry found that school was different from kindergarten. It was a more serious decision. Eileen and Marie were enrolled at Rossbercon, the local private school for girls in Elwood and Harry was sent off to Brighton Grammar School to mix and be educated with boys of his own class. Brighton Grammar had been established in 1882 by George Crowther who was successful in attracting a capable staff and a permanent student population from the sons of professional and mercantile families living in the southeastern suburbs.

By 1924, when Harry Williams enrolled, the school had changed significantly. After Crowther's death in 1918, Brighton Grammar had been put up for sale and early in 1924, a number of local individuals raised the money to purchase the school. A Council, with representatives from the School as an incorporated body, the Vestry of St Andrew's Church and the Old Boy's Society, was formed. Under the direction of the Council, an extensive building program was undertaken and a new school, a gymnasium and the construction of two ovals replaced the collection of little buildings.

The Prospectus promised that boys entering the Lower School at five guineas a term would be provided with an education specially adapted to their needs and religious instruction of a strictly undenominational kind. Sport, too, had a high profile. In 1891, George Crowther had been instrumental in establishing the Victorian Amateur Athletics Association. However, in 1911, anxieties about the amateur status of some of the students who competed led Crowther to organise a breakaway group of schools as the Schools Amateur Athletics Association of Victoria so as to maintain and advance the amateur tradition.

When Harry pulled on his long socks and Doll knotted his tie for him, set his cap with its embossed shield on his head, she stood back and admired him. Harry knew he was clearly defined. Brighton Grammar was a private school not a State School where he had seen boys and girls run and push each other out of the way, using language he knew would have shocked his mother. They all dressed in motley garments and there were even children with no shoes.

On the other hand, Harry knew that Brighton Grammar, although sound, was not the acme of educational status. It lacked the prestige of the six major public schools that attracted the sons of the most prominent residents of the suburb. Eric and Doll were well aware that had they been higher on the social rung, they would have looked to Melbourne Grammar as a possibility for their boy. So there Harry was, embarking on acquiring new skills and new competencies, but, already in the thinking of 1920s Melbourne neatly pigeonholed by his residential address and his choice of school.

Harry was enrolled in the Preparatory School, which served boys from the age of eight to eleven. Two women teachers organised the school and male teachers from the Senior School appeared for certain lessons. When Harry was twelve he moved into the Senior School which promised separate classrooms for each form and a separate desk and seat for each boy.

In February 1927, the new school buildings were opened. Harry lined up with all the other boys to watch the Headmaster with the Anglican Archbishop of Melbourne, the Governor-General and his wife walk up the drive to the official dais. After interminable speeches in which they were told how fortunate they were, the boys dispersed, the rest of the day declared a holiday. Brighton Grammar School was extolled in the newspapers as the epitome of a desirable education.

While the curriculum was important, parents placed emphasis on the social and moral values their boys would learn at school. Religious Instruction was an integral part of the school and in addition to a record of lessons, a report on conduct and attendance was compiled each week. The School exhorted parents to sign this record each week *as it furnishes the best indication of a boy's progress*. Sport was the other way in which boys would learn correct values. Harry's attendance for football and cricket was mandatory - there was a separate field for the junior boys - and there was a program of daily exercises, a new gymnasium and two asphalt tennis courts to use when the weather was good.

Harry's formal learning was heavily oriented to England. Although Anzac may have given impetus to a sense of national identity, within the education system, England was the source of all that was good and wise. As Harry moved through the grades, at every turn, he was confronted by the power of the British Empire. History was a litany of dates and events that made the Empire great, Geography a list of countries and their products that created the trading patterns of Empire and English Literature stories and poetry of English heroes and heroines. World War I had been an unhappy interruption but now all was back in place and the Empire was once again at peace. Each story was to be taken as inspiration for a life of achievement. Harry's understanding was of the power of England as the hub of the Empire that stretched in red across every continent on the globe and embraced Australia in its comforting folds.

Each twenty-fourth of May, the school celebrated Empire Day when the boys would assemble and march to an official reception point to hear the Mayor extol the virtues of the Royal family, the Royal Navy and that

Australia was British to the bootstraps, at least 98% so. A few prayers, some singing - God Save the King, Land of Hope and Glory, Rule Britannia and an Australian offering, the latter sung with much less gusto - and the dignitary would announce a half-holiday. As the benign face of George V graced the pennies Harry's grandmother in Brunswick gave him when they visited her, the bonds of Empire held some currency. It was associated with money and what it could buy - a penny worth of licorice was very acceptable.

As for the 2% who weren't of British background in Australia, they rarely entered Harry's horizons. Stories of World War I centred mainly on Gallipoli and the stereotypes of brave Belgium, militaristic Germany, difficult France and flamboyant Italy, largely dismissing Europe as a colourful but powerless part of the world. Members of the Royal family might holiday there but would never live there permanently. The Irish were nearly British but were beyond the pale because they were Roman Catholic. Harry learned that being a Catholic meant mandatory church attendance on Sundays, whatever, and that a close relationship with a Catholic would entail *turning*. When they were visiting, he sometimes heard the adults discussing a family in the neighbourhood who looked Jewish and were, it was clear, off-limits as playmates.

To Harry, the world was British. The story of the Boston Tea Party showed the residents of the new colonies in America to be unreasonable. George III, who was only trying to reach an agreement and who was so hurt by the loss of the colonies emerged as the hero and the colonists, the villains. As a result of this incident, the American colonies had moved away from the British way and, like the children down the street with whom he was not allowed to play, Americans were now considered to be like us but too wealthy and too loud. The wealth they squandered and their loudness was definitely not the way to do things.

Aside from the heavy diet of Empire, the curriculum at Brighton Grammar was relatively limited in the mid-1920s. Faced with a heavy building debt, the headmaster, Herbert Dixon concentrated on promoting the school, as preparing boys for a commercial career and *the School became a nursery for accountants*. To some parents, this was seen as being at the expense of a more academic education. Chemistry was dropped in 1925 because it was too expensive to offer as a subject and results in the Public Examinations were poor. In the Intermediate examinations that the boys usually sat when they were fourteen, in 1925, three out of twenty-three candidates qualified, in 1931, seventeen out of twenty-seven and in 1932, twenty-one out of forty-nine. Those seeking entry to Melbourne University left for Melbourne Grammar and Scotch College. Towards the end of the decade, as people's finances came under pressure, unpaid fees increased from £36 in 1927 to £850 in 1930.

But Harry did not trouble himself with such concerns for he did not see his future as a lawyer or an accountant. Harry, through his days at Brighton Grammar, tended to blend into the anonymous rows of boys who were neither academic nor in the First Eleven but that gave no trouble. Their future was often determined more by the network of friendships they established than their participation in the classroom or at the wicket.

For most children, growing up in Brighton in the 1920s was a happy experience. Harry was no exception. Brighton was not a suburb of battlers. Life in the pleasant tree-lined streets was ordered and bountiful. At home, Harry, as the only child of prosperous parents, was unencumbered by chores or other domestic responsibilities. There were constant visits to Head Street for Harry and his cousin Eileen or Nob as the families called her were good friends. At weekends and on holidays, when he was there, he would join in the games of the two girls. Often, however, he was left in the company of the home help and the succession of family pet dogs. Harry was not unhappy with this situation for he had early learned to occupy himself with his own toys and games and in the security of his home this was entirely satisfying. At Birdswood Avenue, a billiard table dominated one of the rooms and absorbed hours of his attention.

Then, there was the wireless. Harry was fascinated when it was installed in the lounge room. Although it looked just like another piece of furniture, closer inspection revealed dials and knobs and a speaker, through which the sound emerged. Sometimes the voices crackled and broke up but usually they were loud and clear. In winter, Harry's days came to be regulated by the wireless as much as by school. At five o'clock, he would be lying on the floor for Children's Hour to be followed by the serials - Flash Gordon and The Air Adventures of Jimmy Allen - and then Doll would call him to come and eat his dinner. For the rest of the time, Doll filled the house with the sounds of Tiptoe Thru the Tulips, Swanee and Tea for Two. On Sundays, she shivered at the solemn sermons, turned the wireless off and declared they must get out and go for a drive.

Harry generally thought Doll the best mother a boy could have and compared the mothers of his friends unfavourably to his own. Doll never disciplined him. If he needed an extra threepence or sixpence for some purchase, she would give it to him. If he couldn't find his jumper, she would look for it. If he complained that he was tired, she would tell him to rest while she ran the errand. Harry enjoyed her fussing around him, asking after every minute of his day and giving him a running commentary on her own.

It was Doll who broke the routine of his days by organising some pleasurable activity. She would meet Harry with the announcement that they were off to the pictures. They would go to the local cinema where

Doll would buy tickets in the dress circle and together they would wait expectantly for the Wurlitzer to appear through the floor. Sometimes they went into the city, to the Capitol, with its fantastic stalactite ceiling which opened in 1924 and later, the lavishly decorated Regent and the largest of them all, the State.

The black and white melodramas that flickered on the screen with the pianist cascading through the tender moments and vamping wildly to suggest high drama enthralled them. Doll liked the pictures with names like 'The Heart Specialist' at the Capitol or the Metro-Goldwyn production, 'Confessions of a Queen'. Through them they followed the inevitability of the leading lady recovering from the scoundrel's machinations to fall into the arms of the urbane hero. Sometimes they would go to films especially for Harry - 'Peter Pan', Charlie Chaplin in 'The Gold Rush' and Rin-Tin-Tin, the wonder dog in 'Jaws of Steel'.

Afterwards, there would be a treat at the tearooms. At Hillier's, a chocolate milkshake or a spider - the fizz of lemonade or ginger beer, the scoop of vanilla icecream - to be stirred into a creamy froth or savoured separately when the liquid had been noisily sucked dry. Sometimes they went to Buckley's and had waffles and maple syrup. In summer, there were small fans on each of the tables and Harry would put his head up close to get the cool stream of air on his face.

Harry liked the intimacy of the occasion. Despite Doll's reticence to puncture the decorum of polite society, it was quite acceptable for her to touch up her make-up after afternoon tea. Harry was fascinated with the ritual that was usually conducted only in the most personal confines of his parent's bedroom. It seemed to him that Doll carried around with her the contents of her dressing table in her handbag. First she would snap open the compact and squint into the mirrored lid. Then coat the powder puff and carefully dust her nose, cheeks and forehead before finally jutting out her chin and nose for a last pat. Lipstick was next. Doll favoured the more dramatic colours and applying scarlet to lips at first pursed, then widened and then smacked together demanded close attention. With her face *on*, Doll would turn and ask his approval.

Doll was not demanding of Harry. She had clear ideas of what constituted a social outing and dedicated herself with enthusiasm to the business of deciding where to go, what to wear, when to leave, who to meet. One thing she never worried about was how much it would cost for Doll considered this to be of no concern to her. They were wealthy and able to do as they pleased. Ideas of thrift were alien to her thinking. In their excursions to the pictures, into the city for a shopping expedition or further afield, Harry prepared for the event to unfold as Doll decreed. Doll knew how to have a good time.

If Harry had a privileged life, he still had to learn to deal with the personal relationships of his family. As the decade advanced, Eric and Doll's marriage came under increasing strains. The death of Joan, rather than bringing them together, widened their differences. Eric, who had been often morose in the past, now drank more. And when he had been drinking, he could be violent. Harry never knew when Eric's rages or one of Doll's moods would erupt into a full-blown row. Then, he would sneak away to his bedroom and wait until the worst had subsided and the house would breathe again. One day, Doll turned up at Queenie's with Harry in tow, seeking refuge from her husband. They stayed away for several months before an armistice was arranged and they returned to Eric, now penitent and ready to make amends.

To Harry, Eric was often to be feared. A large man with a deep voice, Eric believed, like many of his generation, in the maxim spare the rod and spoil the child. But Doll, especially with the death of Joan, was very protective of her only child. Sometimes it was, *Harry come out here*, in a thundering voice as Eric found some major transgression had been committed. Since Eric wore braces, he had no belt on the ready. Instead, he would send Harry to the bathroom to bring him the razor strop that hung behind the door. Doll would hover anxiously in the background, defending Harry. *Eric, don't hurt him. Don't hurt him. He's only little.* When Harry, now howling, was allowed to escape, Doll was there to gather him in her arms and soothe his tears. To Harry, the chastisements became intermingled with anxious images of his father, the slamming of the front door and the ominous silence as Eric cast his eye round for something that offended. In Harry's mind, such punishments were not related to him because he had failed to be a responsible member of the household but because of the bad temper of his father.

Between the sometimes heavy hand of his father and the indulgence of his mother, Harry found that, if he weathered the stormy periods, he could negotiate his own path in the daily routines of the home by keeping his own counsel and staying clear when he discerned the danger signs. Harry acquired a reputation for being a quiet boy. Harry was also considered to be a pleasant boy. He rarely made excessive demands on his parent's largesse but, at the same time, there was nothing he wanted that he was not provided with. There was every likelihood that this state of affairs would continue.

In 1928, when Harry was thirteen, his grandfather Williams died. At the funeral, Harry, as the oldest grandson, was appraised much like a young colt and his future discussed. It could only be rosy. Henry Williams had left an estate worth £31,500. The house, 'Nalang' in East Brunswick, the car - a Minerva - and a life interest in his shares and investments that included a two-story Elizabeth Street property went to his wife for her life. The assets would then pass to Eric and Thelma respectively. He left to Eric directly, the Brunswick iron foundry in Weston Street and monies due on a loan. In 1928, for the Williams family, this was a pleasing cushion against the exigencies of a worsening financial situation.

5

It was observed at Henry Williams's funeral that although young Harry had little to say about a future occupation, he brightened up considerably when called on to talk about his hobbies. He liked golf and, according to his father, paternal pride aside, Harry was most promising. It was surprising that, although Harry was right-handed in other things, he was left-handed at golf. The relatives were impressed and they promised to look out for his name in the newspapers.

Harry was to be to the foremost in the generation of young men who changed the face of golf in Melbourne between the wars. In the decades of the 1920s and 1930s, golf's popularity changed the appearance of the sport considerably. However, the earlier view of golf as providing the facilities of a gentlemen's club and as the natural province of the amateur continued to exert a strong influence.

In the late nineteenth century, golf was organised as a recreation for the gentlemen and the ladies of the colony. In 1891, a number of individuals - men of influence and substance - subscribed fifteen guineas each to establish the Melbourne Golf Club at Caulfield. Golf Clubs were formed at Geelong, Surrey Hills, Essendon and Kew in the succeeding years. As much as possible, founding members attempted to replicate Scottish links in the Australian setting. In March 1903, a group of Melbourne businessmen gathered at the Port Phillip Hotel in Flinders Street to discuss forming a golf club at Sandridge. They selected the land because it possessed *many of the golfing characteristics of the coastal courses of the old country.*

Once on the links, golf, it was thought, was a mind game. Horace G. Hutchinson, who in 1890 produced the volume on *Golf* for the Badminton Library of Sport and Pastimes edited by His Grace the Duke of Beaufort and dedicated to His Royal Highness The Prince of Wales, saw the game as a pleasing complement to a professional life. *To play it aright requires nerve, endurance, and self-control, qualities which are essential to success in all great vocations.*

The act of placing oneself in a humbling situation was considered a salutary experience for the powerful. From this period of the game, a vocabulary relating to poor players was coined: to foozle, the act of foozling, to be a foozler or a rabbit all referred to unskilled golf. Indeed, in 1901, when the Victorian Lieutenant-Governor and Chief Justice, Sir John Madden, opened the new Royal Melbourne course at Sandringham, he distinguished himself as a foozler, first with a fresh air shot and then with his next that dribbled only a few yards. Sir John joined in the laughter.

For many men, as the golf club was an extension of their business lives, they declared that women would inhibit their enjoyment there. Daniel Soutar, who published *The Australian Golfer*, the first instructional book on golf in Australia in 1906, recommended that *women with a handicap of not more than five strokes should, I think, be allowed to play over the men's courses at will, except on Saturdays and public holidays, it being understood that they would always be willing to allow men, coming on behind, to pass them, if the latter so desire.* While women might be acknowledged on the course, they could never be treated as equal in the clubhouse. After all, strong language, topics relating to sensitive matters and male camaraderie would be severely curtailed if they appeared there. It was not until 1925, for instance, that women members were admitted to Victoria Golf Club and even then, with limits set on their access to facilities.

Golf also clearly carried the concept of the golf club member as employer and the professional and caddie as employees. There was a strict division between member and professional. Clubs appointed professionals to make golf clubs for members, to teach them to play the game and to sell them golfing accessories. Often professionals were brought over from Scotland. They were required to defer to members at all times. They could also be requested to play a round with members and be part of a betting team but not to follow members into the clubhouse and bar.

Caddies were even more strictly controlled. Caddies, usually boys looking to earn pocket money, carried the bag of clubs for the member. There was a caddie master and usually a caddie compound where the boys waited until their services were required. Apart from his commission, at most Golf Clubs, the caddie master could earn extra money by cleaning member's boots and undertaking other odd jobs. Although professionals and caddies may have joked about the members to each other, theirs was essentially a Master and Servant relationship.

Most significantly, golf courses were established as Clubs. The *Australasian* of 24 June 1893 reported that *at the close of the play the competitors in twos make for the club-house and the bankers, merchants, and barristers resume the habits and speech of civilised life to discuss the incidents of the day and apply the law to doubtful cases*. This was the Nineteenth Hole. As A. D. Ellis in his 1941 history of Royal Melbourne Golf Club asserted, it was *the most important hole of all. ... To fail at the Nineteenth is unpardonable; it denotes a lack of one or other of those instincts which, when combined, constitute camaraderie and good fellowship*. A tradition of sportsmanship, hospitality and good fellowship was established. At Royal Melbourne, members enjoyed a dressing room, a smoking room, a reading room, a library, a dining room and, of course, a bar. When new golf clubs were formed, clubhouses were as important to members as the establishment of a course.

For many members, the golf club doubled as their gentlemen's club. When the rest of Melbourne society found its drinking habits seriously under attack from an alliance of temperance, religious and political groups at the turn of the century, golf clubs escaped unscathed. In 1915, the Victorian government limited trading hours from 9 a.m. to 9.30 p.m. and in 1916, reduced them further to 6 p.m. Golf clubs had to conform with the legislation but used a variety of strategies to moderate its worst features. At Riversdale Golf Club, according to Joe Johnson, the Club applied for their licence under an 1850s Act that gave them immunity from sudden police raids. In 1920, the Royal Melbourne Golf Club, threatened with further restrictions, took the case to the Supreme Court and won. In this scenario, golf was leisure and within the freedom of a private club, away from the public wowserism of Melbourne society, members created a congenial environment. This also applied to the playing of golf on Sundays, an activity publicly criticised but pursued by members with impunity.

Although there were some changes to the organisation of golf in the first decades of the twentieth century, it was during the 1920s that significant changes occured. Of these changes, Harry Williams was both a catalyst and a beneficiary. On one hand, it was the suburban expansion along the bay that encouraged the establishment of golf clubs and on the other, boys like Harry found the expanded opportunities to play golf irresistible. Unlike some Australian writers such as George Johnson or Graham McInnes, who felt oppressed by the uniformity of southeastern suburbia, for Harry and his friends the area held the magical worlds of the golf course. Behind the fences, landscaped vistas delighted the eye and offered walks in a most beautiful construction of nature. Fairways of mown grass edged by trees and bushes led the eye to a flag and the symmetry of a small circle set in a smooth green: an enchanting combination that conferred desirability on an otherwise flat and uneventful urban development.

Already, the potential of the area to the southeast of the city had been recognised. Royal Melbourne Golf Club and Metropolitan Golf Club had moved to new golf courses in the area that came to be known as the sandbelt by World War I. After the war, the process accelerated, especially when the affluence of the 1920s encouraged clubs to expand their horizons. The Commonwealth Golf Club, Kingston Heath Golf Club, Victoria Golf Club and Yarra Yarra Golf Club all established fine courses on the sandbelt during the decade.

The interest in golf widened. Contemporaries called it a craze. On some golf courses, a contest for the space emerged. Joe Johnson, in *Birdies and Billabongs: a history of the Kew Golf Club* tells of the secretary's problems in 1921. The secretary reported that complaints had reached him from several members regarding the number of hoodlums who were now infesting the course on Sundays. Most of them were armed with a club of some sort and played over the course in batches of half dozen to a dozen and frequently got in the way of members. Their language also was not up to golfers' standards for the member wrote: *I have again to draw your attention to the dreadful manner in which the links are overrun by young men and boys on Sunday mornings. They steal your golf balls, jeer at you, and swear at you in the most disgusting manner I ever heard. I may state that yesterday morning when my partner and I frustrated three youths in stealing our golf balls, they jeered at us, and when our backs were turned they pelted us with dung, and when I thanked them for their attention the language they hurled at me could have set the Yarra on fire.* A firm of private detectives was hired to *keep the links clear of the hoodlum element.*

Public courses were established. In 1925, Brighton Council opened a 9-hole public course and in the first three months, takings amounted to £180. In 1928, an 18-hole public course was opened at Yarra Bend. At Elsternwick, the swamp, first known as the Elsternwick Common, and occupying the square bounded by Glenhuntly Road, and St Kilda, New and Head Streets was originally withheld from sale. In 1880, a trotting track had been formed and operated there for ten years. In 1891, it was forced to move out to Oakleigh through the efforts of a group of residents backed by the Honourable Sir Frederick Sargood of Ripponlea who objected to the disruption of race days and to the sport itself. These concerned residents found golf to be a suitable replacement and in the mid-1890s, an eighteen-hole golf course was laid out and a golf club formed. In 1925, because of the competition for sporting space in the municipality, the lease was terminated; the golf course was reduced to nine holes and cricket, football, rugby, soccer and hockey fields were laid out on land occupied by the other nine holes.

Golf, generally, became more commercial. In the early 1920s, the wooden tee peg superseded the little mound of sand from the tee box and along with golf balls became the ultimate consumer item, constantly requiring renewal. Although professionals continued to make and repair golf clubs, sports companies began to take an increased interest in manufacturing and supplying equipment. In 1922, Arthur Spence, writing in *Golf*, recorded the arrival of the first batch of numbered, graded iron heads to Melbourne and in 1926, the Spalding brothers located a plant in Melbourne. In order to sell their products, Spalding and Dunlop, through advertising, spread the word that golf was not a rich person's sport but was accessible to all.

Opportunities for tournament competition increased. Club championships and state and national titles formed the basis of the golfing calendar. The expansion of pennant competition over the 1920s brought more players into elite competition. During the 1890s, as clubs were formed, competition began as inter-club challenges and in 1899 a pennant competition was formed. By 1926, the inclusion of Yarra Yarra, Kingston Heath, Commonwealth and Woodlands into the senior pennant lists required the formation of two divisions. Then, the calendar of major events was increased with events such as the *Australasian* Foursomes Cup while more clubs began to organise events such as the Sorrento Cup on the Australia Day weekend or the Riversdale Cup on the King's Birthday weekend that attracted fields of top golfers.

With the expansion of interest in golf, the standard of the sport improved. Certainly, there were good golfers in the early decades but in the ten years before World War I, the average winning score in the Australian Open was 317.8 whereas in the decade after the war, the average winning score dropped to 299.3, a difference of 18.5 strokes. The new players began to make an impact. Jack Dillon, writing in his column in *The Sporting Globe* on the state of golf in Australia, observed that the businessmen, lawyers and doctors were now overshadowed. *On the links the leaders of industry and stars of professions, still get as much pleasure as in the days that were, but more often their staffs, and often enough their mere messenger boys, completely outshine them in golf skill.* Indeed, Dillon continued, *most of the best players we have, and the holders of club and other titles, are young men, many of whom have graduated from the ranks of caddies.*

There remained, however, several sources of tension in Australian golf. Despite the success of golf in the United States and of American and British professionals, Australian golf clubs continued to look to the Royal and Ancient Golf Club of St Andrew's for leadership and to award the highest accolades to the amateur player. In 1921, the Royal and Ancient and the United States Golf Association agreed to a standard ball size. In 1931, however, the USGA shifted to a larger ball. The smaller British ball remained the standard for Australia. In scoring, bogey, which was represented by the very British imaginary figure of a Colonel, remained standard until the early 1930s. In 1924, when steel-shafted clubs were accepted for championship play by the USGA, the Royal and Ancient

Golf Club maintained its ban until 1929. In the process, change often took even longer to occur in Australian golf than in Britain.

But more complex was the division between amateur and professional golfers. From the beginning of organised competition, greater status was accorded to amateur competition. In 1894, the first Australian Championship was held, only for amateurs. If the Australian Championship was to showcase the best golfers in the nation, there emerged the argument that professional golfers should be included. In 1904, the first Australian Open Championship was held, allowing both professionals and amateurs to compete. Yet professionals were not accorded full recognition. They remained outside the inner sanctums of the clubhouse even when competing in the same event. Moreover, on two occasions, in 1907 and 1912, the amateurs Michael Scott and Ivo Whitton, won the Open on rulings of play to the detriment of professionals. In both cases, professional golfers argued that discrimination motivated the decision.

More generally, golf increasingly entered the sporting culture of Melbourne and the Williams household. All the newspapers carried columns on golf and employed regular writers to attract readers: Hugh Anderson in the *Argus*, Harry Culliton in *The Australasian*, Earl Robieson in the *Sun News Pictorial*, Jack Dillon in *The Sporting Globe*, Gus Jackson in *Table Talk*. Magazines such as *Golf and Tennis in Australia* appeared specifically addressed to the growing market. The advertisements for Dewars Whisky, Drummond & Co Watches and Jewellery, Catanach's Diamond Rings and Southern Motors implied that golfers were still considered to be amongst the wealthier in the society.

Golfing celebrities appeared. Joe Kirkwood, as an Australian, captured headlines as a major star with a flair for publicity. In 1920, Joe Kirkwood, professional at the Riversdale Golf Club, won the Australian Open and the New Zealand Open Championships. In the following year, golfers raised £1,000 to send Kirkwood to the British Open where he finished fourth. By 1923, Kirkwood had embarked on another phase of his career. He took up the position of professional at the Rockwood Country Club, New York and from there, travelled the world demonstrating his amazing skills as a golfing showman. In the Williams household, Joe Kirkwood received close attention from Harry and Eric. Joe Kirkwood was like an aviator - he popped up in all parts of the world, pictured nonchalantly hitting huge distances with balls resting in apparently unplayable lies. One of his more bizarre shots was to use a person to rest the golf ball on. But most significantly, an Australian had become rich and famous through playing golf.

Although the expansion of the courses indicated the widening popularity of golf as a sport, in Melbourne, golf was still often seen as an adjunct to a business life. When Stanley Bruce, the Prime Minister, officially opened Victoria Golf Club in 1927, he stated he was delighted to see the game expanding because the qualities necessary for success in golf were identical to those needed to build a nation. A column in the *Herald* in July 1929 entitled How Our Busy Men Keep Fit placed golf as the chief recreation for those at the top, from Supreme Court judges to Chief Commissioners to the Prime Minister. It was claimed that *a great many men who slip away from the office to the golf course claim to do so out of a stern sense of duty. Golf, they say, is essential to the proper performance of their onerous jobs.* In the 1920s, memberships to Melbourne Cricket Club, to Royal Melbourne or Metropolitan Golf Clubs and enrolment at Melbourne Church of England Grammar School were still the most desirable gifts a father could give his son at birth.

This, then, was the situation of golf in Melbourne in the 1920s when Harry Williams, responding to the wide range of cultural influences, decided that he would investigate the game. He would take out a golf club and, placing a golf ball on the ground, swing the club back and then striking the ball sweetly send it soaring into eternity. There was still much to do, but from the first swing, Harry knew that here was something he did exceptionally well.

6

While other boys growing up in the suburbs along Port Phillip Bay spent endless hours at the beach, dive-bombing from the Middle Brighton pier did not take Harry's fancy. Instead, it was the open spaces that still remained between the houses that attracted his attention. Using the clumps of tea-tree as obstacles, and largely oblivious to the wildflowers that appeared in spring, Harry and his friends devised impromptu golf courses. When Harry was eleven, Eric, who was a keen golfer and had a battery of golf clubs at home, took him down to the public course at Brighton for a game.

At school, Harry had found a good friend in Harold Edward Richard (Dick) Payne, whose father owned a large drapery store in Gardenvale. Born in December 1911, Dick was three and a half years older than Harry. When Harry had started in the Prep School, Dick as one of the older Prep boys shared a common classroom and play area. Harry's friendship with Dick Payne flourished as they both experimented with playing golf.

Soon, the boys were sufficiently proficient to seek out a golf course. From Brighton Grammar on the Outer Crescent, it was only a mile as the crow flew to the southern end of the Elsternwick course. It was close too to Harry's successive homes and before or after school Harry would meet up with Dick or Alex Rae, another boy their age, for a hit of golf. Once there, they would slip on to the course at the 2nd tee through the wire fence, play until the 17th and then disappear before they reached the clubhouse. Boys, keen to play golf, were indulged and Bill Uren, who was a member at Victoria but also played at Elsternwick, remembered teaming up with them on various occasions. In this way, older men inducted boys into the sport, waiving the fees in favour of encouraging them to play the game.

Boys like Harry and Dick, with a couple of clubs and a putter, honed their skills around the public courses. Then, they often looked to a private club where they could earn a shilling or two caddying for the members. Indeed, so endemic was the popularity of golf that, in 1928, the Victorian Education Department issued an edict concerning boys acting as caddies and being absent from school. Usually, the caddies were invited to take part in an annual event organised for them by the club. Success in the event was a major step, some chose to make a career in golf at this point and became apprenticed to professionals as their assistants. Others were selected by clubs to become junior members at reduced fees in order to encourage them in playing the game. Generally, this policy was used to fast-track the admission of *better* golfers produced by the independent schools that played golf as part of senior sport.

Over these years, Harry forged his own understanding of how to play golf. He asked Doll to buy him all the magazines and books available on golf and he pored over them in his search for helpful advice. He studied photographs of the leading overseas players with the idea of learning how they obtained their length, their accuracy and so on. From Tommy Armour, World Champion, he learned to hit from inside out and to take the club back as low to the ground as possible. For the best putting style, Harry modelled himself on Walter Hagen, always to putt from the front foot.

But most importantly, Harry sought direction on strategy. In his scrapbook, Harry pasted two articles by J. H. Taylor, the British Open champion. One gave mundane but necessary advice on water hazards; the other offered a philosophy of golf. It was entitled Those Who

Experiment Enjoy the Game. After arguing that golfers should be confident in shot-making Taylor had concluded, *there will always remain a wide gulf between the tigers and the rabbits*. Harry decided he would be amongst the tigers. He and Dick gave themselves nicknames - Harry, the Tiger and Dick, the Horse, as images of their golfing philosophy.

To be a tiger, however, required having complete control of the basic skills of golf: grooving out a swing and developing a full repertoire of strokes. On the golf course with Dick or other boys or his father and in the backyard at home, Harry found there was a clear correlation between effort and reward. He would take a club out for hours after school, at weekends and in the holidays. It was eminently satisfying to pitch balls into a target circle he had devised on the couch grass that had been coaxed into a lawn at the back of the house. It was pleasing to try and increase the ratio of balls that went into the various putting gadgets bought by Eric for him to use on the drawing room carpet. Harry even devised several of his own design. Sometimes, the floor looked like a very crowded billiard table. When Harry had been playing and not hitting well with a club, he would go out with a dozen balls and practise for hours on end if necessary to groove a reliable swing.

While Harry, the teenager, dreamt of taking the golf course by boldness, Doll and Eric conceived of his golf in terms related to their own situations. Doll and Eric shared Harry's pleasure in mastering the game. Doll was unquestioning in her support, for Harry's success was also hers. Eric was more ambitious and looked at Harry's style critically. He would come out and stand, frowning, as Harry pitched balls in the backyard, a stern taskmaster. Under his direction, Harry overcame the anxieties occasioned by his father's presence and learned to maintain his own smooth, fluid stroke under the most baleful of gazes. But also, for Doll and Eric, golf was about golf clubs.

44

When Harry entered the Senior School at Brighton Grammar in 1927 and earned the right to wear long trousers, he was already a competent golfer. He played in the Saturday morning competitions at the Elsternwick public course but, in Eric's view, joining a club was essential. Eric made inquiries and in June 1927, Harry Williams was elected as a junior member at Commonwealth Golf Club. Eric also joined.

Over the next two years, Harry learned to be a golfer at Commonwealth. Opened in 1921, the course had matured and its lawn-like fairways and well-kept greens were impeccable after, what one commentator labelled as *the erratic swards of Elsternwick*. The hazards were well devised and maintained to penalise the rabbits and to reward the tigers. Playing competition showed Harry's talent. Given a mark of twenty by the handicapper on joining, Harry reduced this by five and five weeks later by another five.

Eric also intervened in Harry's development by bringing his ideas of discipline to the golf course. One evening, Archie Campbell, assistant professional at Commonwealth, was following Eric and Harry as they played a round of golf. On the 16th, a long hole where water was strategically placed up towards the green, Harry played an iron in around the edge of the lake. Instead of making the green, the ball drifted into a deep bunker. To Archie's amazement, Eric took to Harry with a golf club he had pulled from his bag, hitting him around the shoulders. Then he instructed Harry to drop another ball and to apply himself to the task of reaching the green without error. Archie, feeling for the boy, was relieved when Harry bent to the task and this time the ball dropped on to the green coming to rest a yard or two from the pin.

Eric gained a reputation in the clubhouse. After the day's play, Eric would join members for a drink or two or more, leaving Harry, cold and hungry, waiting in the car. In 1928, when a new clubhouse was opened with extended facilities, Eric became a feature of the bar while Harry remained resentfully outside, sometimes falling asleep before his father decided to leave.

Soon, Harry showed evidence of being more than an ordinary player. On Saturday 21 July 1928, a week after his thirteenth birthday, Harry played in the 9-hole open back markers' morning event at Elsternwick on a handicap of six. He won with a net score of 29. Then, in the afternoon, he presented himself at Commonwealth for the monthly medal played against Bogey.

On Monday, Doll couldn't wait for Eric to bring in the newspaper from the garden where the newspaper boy tossed it early each morning. Risking getting her slippers wet, she brought in the paper to lay it on the breakfast table. Quickly leafing through the pages she found the picture pages and a photograph of Harry - Young Champion of the links – Harry Williams, 13, of Commonwealth Club - and then a fuller account in the sports pages - Boy Golfer Wins Commonwealth Medal. Harry was in print. There, in black and white - 5-4-3 5-5-6 4-3-5 - 40 and 4-4-4 6-3-5 4-3-5 - 38 with the result that he ended four up on Bogey given he was off four. Doll fairly raced around the household tasks so she could go and show Queenie the news.

In golfing circles, Harry's success occasioned comment at Commonwealth. Outside the professional shop on the Monday morning, a number of older members gathered before hitting off.
What did you think of young Harry's win?
Oh, it's just a flash in the pan. You watch him, he won't have the patience when he really gets up against it. I've heard that he's got a temper - that won't help him.
I don't know about that. As far as I hear, that's his father, not Harry. The boy's got great judgment. Ted Hoban was on the tee on the 9th

and he was watching them come up the 8th. He said Harry's got all the shots and plays them with confidence. No, I think he'll go on.
The other golfers demurred for in their mind golf was not just about hitting the ball but tenacity, composure and perseverance, the properties of the mature male only.
Look at the top golfers around. They've proved themselves over and over again. No, golf is best played by ones with experience. Look at Ivo Whitton.
There was general assent.
But Ivo Whitton was only fourteen when he joined at Metropolitan. Well, he's proved himself. This boy Williams might have had a lucky day.
The golfer, who had spoken first persevered, *You can't deny that Williams's actual score was the best of the day. He hits the ball with force and he's straight too. He's only thirteen and these young ones are all giving Bogey a hiding.*
The conversation moved away from Harry to the more vexatious issue of the day, the increased playing of stroke rounds over match play and the playing to par rather than to Bogey.

Organised competition absorbed more hours of Harry's time. In 1929, he was selected in the Commonwealth pennant team. He made his debut against Yarra Yarra and won his first match decisively with a round of 76. Lessons increasingly became the time to be filled before meeting up with Dick and the other boys who played golf around the suburbs. Sometimes school was skipped altogether.

Weekends could be completely devoted to playing. In the holidays, there were still days when Harry went around to the Lake's and he and Eileen would play long games of tennis at the public courts up the street. Harry liked tennis and was always competitive but he would sulk if Eileen beat him.

47

When he was about fourteen, Harry found that his days were extended. He was allowed to go out after dinner. Such licence was strictly curbed, however, by the nightly curfew self-enforced in comfortable Brighton. So it was the pictures at the Prince George - a different diet from those Harry went to with Doll - the same newsreels, cartoons and trailers, but then Westerns and Thrillers. Harry learned to keep up the appearance of confidence as bullets thudded into getaway cars or Indians' arrows whistled by.

In March 1930, Harry received a further important lesson about playing golf. The boys were all talk. The great Walter Hagen and Joe Kirkwood had arrived in Australia. They were like the aviators the boys followed - their tour through southeastern Australia ate up the miles as each day found them at another golf course showing their skills to another appreciative gallery. During March, they appeared at Manly, Killara, the Australian, then down through rural New South Wales, stopping in at Goulburn to amaze the locals on the way. By the middle of March they arrived in Melbourne. The boys followed their every move.

On Saturday 15 March, Hagen and Kirkwood played at Victoria Golf Club and Doll and Eric took Harry and Eileen to watch their exhibition match. The gallery was the biggest ever to follow a round of golf in Melbourne and paid 10/- entry fee for the pleasure. Hagen had an injured thumb but still produced the golf to draw oohs and aahs of admiration. Hagen and Kirkwood were all square after the 18th. On the 19th, Hagen set Kirkwood a stymie. On the putting green, if a player's ball came to rest between the opponent's ball and the hole, the opponent had either to play around the ball or, if skilled enough, to chip over it. Usually, it was at the cost of an extra stroke. Kirkwood studied the stymie carefully but failed to negotiate it, knocking Hagen's ball into the hole with the result that Hagen emerged the winner.

Harry was struck most by Hagen's attitude to the game. What impressed him was Hagen's relaxed approach. On one hole, when his drive ended in the rough, Hagen had strolled over to where his ball lay and had made some wisecrack to his caddie. Harry decided to model himself on Hagen, telling Dick when they met up, *His attitude to the game is the ideal one; he never loses his head, he never gets rattled when things go wrong, he just keeps calm.* But Harry also heard how the great Walter Hagen enjoyed the night life and had arrived at one tournament still dressed in his dinner suit. To a fifteen-year-old, this appeared the height of style.

After the game, while boys like Harry and Dick were out on the course attempting to reproduce shots they had seen, most members retired to the bar to meet the visitors and to consider the day's play. An indication of the conviviality of the occasion was the story told in Don Lawrence's history, *Victoria Golf Club*. At the end of the night, George Dickenson and Jim Fogarty, two Victoria Golf Club members, left later for the weekend at Flinders. On Monday, Jim deposited George at his office but when George phoned his home to organise for someone to bring his car in for him, he was told it wasn't there. He telephoned the police to record it stolen and waited for it to be recovered. Several days passed, but no success. He bought a new car. Then, a week or two later George arranged a game of golf at Victoria and, on driving into the car park, was accosted by one of the employees and asked how long was he going to leave his car in the car park? His car was standing where he had parked it before the Kirkwood-Hagen match.

Such an oversight occasioned much laughter. By contrast, Eric Williams' behaviour at Commonwealth was evoking less sympathy. At the Club, Harry had more to contend with than a reputation as a boy with potential. Eric had blotted his copybook at Commonwealth and was now *persona non grata*. Eric was outraged. Harry must leave the Club too. Dick Payne had joined Victoria Golf Club as a junior member in June 1929 and Harry was happy to move there.

In October 1930, Eric applied for himself and Harry to join Victoria Golf Club. During the 1920s, Victoria Golf Club became an important symbol of status in Melbourne golfing society. In 1922, as the Victoria Golf Club merely leased the land at Sandridge, members began negotiations to purchase 128 acres of land at Cheltenham. Debentures to pay the price of £25,000 for the land were raised and clearing began. It was covered with low-lying scrub, patches of tea-tree and an occasional eucalypt. It had been used for military manoeuvres. In 1926, the world famous golf course architect, Dr Alister Mackenzie, who had been brought to Melbourne by Royal Melbourne Golf Club for their new course, also inspected Victoria for a fee of £200. His advice helped produce a golf course described as *a parkland of natural beauty,* much more in the tradition of the great British landscaped gardens of the eighteenth century than the windswept links of Scotland.

The move to Cheltenham also occasioned the building of a large new clubhouse. Built at the cost of £25,000, it was featured in the magazines of the day. *Table Talk* on 19 May 1927 enthused, *the wonderful new bungalow clubhouse, sumptuously fitted and apportioned for the every comfort of members and associates, is the greatest of its kind in Australia.* In January 1929, the clubhouse was the subject of a feature article in the *Australian Home Beautiful.* Its *air of massive luxury* impressed Kitty McEwan, the writer. It was, she continued, *the nearest approach we have in Victoria at the present time to anything of its kind in America, the home of magnificent clubhouses.* The dining room seated a hundred people and when cleared of furniture allowed for dancing, making the club *one of Melbourne's most attractive dancing rendezvous.* Kitty McEwan observed that this was a departure from convention. *It is only of recent date that social life has made itself felt in the golf world, and in spite of ancient Scottish traditions being against that sort of thing, the Royal and Ancient game has not suffered through the introduction of this attractive intrusion to club life.*

Eric's application of 30 October 1930 to the Victoria Golf Club was refused. His reputation had preceded him. As the Victoria Golf Club directors were at loggerheads with the associates over the associates' rights to control the entry of new members at the time, they were in a difficult position. They were reluctant to complicate life by accepting an applicant with dubious credentials, even though his son may be a very promising player. As well, young people were giving them trouble from another quarter. The caddie master was instructed to make sure that the caddies stayed within their compound and that their use of obscene language must stop. Boys were getting out of hand.

Harry found that playing golf at Commonwealth, boys had to be little gentlemen. When he and Dick and others their age were playing together, they could make extravagant wagers, indulge in horseplay or express their annoyance. But in the more formal context of competition, the veneer of goodwill and companionship had many unwritten rules that Harry learned to recognise. To show frustration, to indulge in a tantrum, to irritate a partner or offend the opposition were unacceptable for anyone. For a youth, such behaviour was worse. They were breaking one of the conditions of their acceptance into the Club, that they were gentlemen. Apparently, on several occasions, this proved insufficient guide to restraint and it was reported that Harry had shown his disappointment. But this was not indicative of Harry's general approach and if, at times, he felt annoyed, Harry remembered the model of Walter Hagen and that casual indifference was the way to move forward.

In 1930, although Harry was instrumental in winning Commonwealth's first senior pennant, he did not gain a reputation for being boastful. Harry found it more diplomatic to be enthusiastic about what others had done for him than to offer information on his own accomplishments. Also, Harry was ready to listen. Young men had to master the rules and etiquette of the game if they were to proceed in its affairs. Over the months,

Harry learned not just to assess each lie carefully, to estimate distance to the pin accurately and to select the best club, but also to mark cards accurately, to sign and date his own card correctly and to make sure his handicap was entered. He also learned etiquette. To avoid problems, Harry found that knowing the rules was worthwhile and to appeal for advice when something untoward occurred. There were many that were prepared to help him for Harry showed exceptional talent.

There were others, however, who were critical of such precocious talent. They were the ones who watched Harry closely for signs of childish temper or for a collapse so that he could be relegated to the ordinary. Another form of censure surfaced in the July 1930 edition of *Tennis and Golf*. It was asserted that schoolboys like Harry Williams and Jim Ferrier should not concentrate on golf. *The main thing to develop character and physique in the adolescent is the good old-fashioned school team games... Football, to our way of thinking, is the game for the growing boy. That's the game to knock the nonsense out of him.* Boys, up till the age of eighteen, it was recommended, should concentrate on school games. *To be quite candid, boys are not very popular on golf courses. Men like to mix with men in their moments of relaxation.*

The last months of 1930 marked the end of Harry's schooldays. In September, as a suitable finale, he played in the first Victorian Boys' championship held at Victoria Golf Club for boys under eighteen where he was runner-up. In December, at the age of fifteen, he bade goodbye to Brighton Grammar School. He did this without regret. He was no scholar. Over his schooldays, Doll and Eric applied little pressure on him to improve his marks or to stay on. Both were happy with his success at golf. Through golf, they thought, Harry was learning the lessons of life. They were also confident that they were comfortably wealthy so Harry need not get a job immediately.

7

By the winter of 1930, when Harry joined the ranks of the elite golfers in Melbourne and began to challenge its leaders, Melbourne was deeply divided by the stresses of Depression. Evictions became the site for battles between the unemployed and landlords and meetings and demonstrations thrust the issues into the public arena. In July, Sir Otto Niemeyer arrived to report on the nation's financial affairs and the popular cry to repudiate Australia's war debts sent shock waves through members of the golf clubs of the sandbelt. Sir Otto fitted in rounds of golf at Royal Melbourne and Metropolitan and went to the races at Flemington. His report to tighten the belt and reduce wages appeared to many to reflect an indifference to the ordinary person's problems.

Eric and Doll may have joined in anxious talk about the militancy of the unemployed, but their lives were untouched by hardship. In 1931, Harry applied himself to playing golf at the topmost level with little awareness of the difficulties being experienced in households throughout the city. He played in the Club pennant, entered the major events of the golfing calendar and hoped to peak for the state championships and the national championships to be held in Sydney in the spring.

To Harry, two events marked his graduation into serious golf. In 1930, Harry had won the Riversdale Open event, beating players like Alex Russell and Mick Ryan. Then, in January 1931, he won the Sorrento Open meeting, defeating most of the leading Melbourne amateurs and professionals with a score of 72 and 76. After winning once or twice in strong fields, he was confident his swing was sound and that he could remain focussed over an extended playing period. These successes also launched Harry's public life. Although the newspaper reports of winning the monthly medal at Commonwealth in 1928 had been dramatic, it was his youthfulness that most appealed. Now, victories in two important events within months indicated more than just juvenile enthusiasm. Henceforth, golf journalists made sure they looked for Harry's name in events and some of the men playing on Monday mornings at Commonwealth indulged in *I told you so*.

However, Harry's membership status remained unresolved. In January 1931, he applied again to Victoria but was told that junior membership was full. On 20 July, Harry resigned from Commonwealth, expecting to be admitted as a junior member at Victoria where he had again applied. But on 30 July, the Victoria directors met, discussed the application and again turned it down. A fortnight passed and yet another application from Harry Williams appeared before the Victoria board seeking junior membership. This time, on 13 August, it was agreed that Harry's name be placed on the board for election. However, a fortnight later, opposition to his nomination was again raised and held over for further discussion on his acceptability.

While the directors at Victoria Golf Club debated the characters of Harry and his father, Eric, they were also concerned by the financial situation. Golf clubs that had invested heavily during the 1920s were generally in some degree of difficulty. In July 1931, when the Governor-General made a public announcement that he would take a 25% reduction in salary and allowances, a special finance sub-committee was formed to examine and make recommendations on Victoria Golf Club finances. The Club still owed a substantial amount for the establishment of the course at Cheltenham and they now attempted to negotiate a new agreement, halving their annual repayments and paying less interest on members' debentures. There were retrenchments of staff and, of those who remained, all wages were reduced: the bar steward, 'Jock', 'Norman', Cook, the three waitresses and the kitchen maid.

These events passed Harry by. Instead, he was caught up with meeting and getting to know a circle of golfers who, at different times, were opposition, partners or team members. They were all different ages and different personalities who, while not necessarily best friends, were bound together by spending hours in each others company. Over the next decade, they would become more intimately known to Harry than many of his relatives.

At Victoria, there was Dick Payne, who continued to be Harry's most constant playing partner during the week. Dick was painstaking in his ambition to improve his golf. He sought lessons from the club professional and adopted a deliberate, careful approach to playing each shot, especially his putting. He was also a good friend and Harry, never very talkative, found him a useful sounding board for airing his concerns about golf and life in general.

There were a number of young men who were, like Harry, part of the post war boom in golf. M.J. (Mick) Ryan, now in his early thirties, was a member at Kingston Heath. In his earlier years, Mick devoted his attention to playing cricket and football for South Melbourne. He was an agile forward and a member of the 1918 premiership team. Mick carried his coordination into golf. In 1927, he turned to golf as his major sporting interest and came to be regarded as one of the best stylists of the orthodox sort in Australia. Mick Ryan won the Australian Amateur title in 1929 and the Victorian Amateur title in 1930. He enjoyed a reputation for sportsmanship and was one of the most popular figures in the game. Although he was stated to be a timber broker, Mick was able to largely devote himself to playing golf.

A.W. (Gus) Jackson was at Victoria. Gus, also in his thirties, had begun golf hitting around with his cousin, Mick Ryan, at Victoria when it was still at Sandridge. At the age of ten, he had won a caddies' tournament, playing with a driver, mashie and mid-iron. Then he played at Royal Park before he was nominated for membership at Victoria by Bill Meader who had recognised his talent. Gus became a member at Sandridge and set its course record. With the move to Cheltenham, Gus dominated the club championships throughout the 1920s and established the course record there as well. In 1926 he won the Victorian Amateur Championship. Gus wrote golfing columns in the *Sun News Pictorial* and *Table Talk* in the period and offered thoughtful observations on the game in Victoria.

Bill Edgar, born in Yarrawonga in 1909, was another youthful prodigy. When his family moved to Melbourne, Bill immediately joined in the enthusiasm for golf in his new neighbourhood. Together with a group of boys, Bill laid out their own 9-hole course on the open paddocks at the corner of Warrigal and North Roads in Oakleigh. He also began as a caddie, carrying for Bob Hancock at Metropolitan. When Bill Edgar joined Commonwealth in 1925, his first handicap was four that he soon reduced to scratch. In 1927 he won the Victorian Amateur Championship.

The recognised older golfers that Harry met largely came from Royal Melbourne, the dominant pennant power at the time. The Club's most effective winner was Ivo Whitton, born in 1893. Ivo Whitton, while at Melbourne Grammar started hitting golf balls around the open paddocks at Armadale where he lived. When he was fourteen, Ivo joined Metropolitan and by the time he was 16 he was playing at number one in their pennant team. He moved to Royal Melbourne Golf Club and gained employment in the Lempriere wool business where the off-season allowed him time to play in the main golfing events of the year. In the 1920s, however, he went to work for Spalding and began that happy association between sporting goods companies and players that sustained the convention of the amateur sportsman.

Ivo Whitton, by the early 1930s, was the elder statesman of Melbourne golf. From 1919 to 1924, Whitton won five out of the six Victorian Amateur Championships, the Australian Amateur Championship in 1922 and 1923 and the Australian Open in 1926 and 1929. Whitton cultivated his own style - he played with six favourite clubs - a brassie (2-wood), a cleek (4-wood), a mid-iron (3-iron), a mashie (5-iron), a lofter (7- or 8-iron also called a niblick) and a putter - and in a distinctive floppy felt hat. Syd Dalrymple and Alex Russell also played at Royal Melbourne, the latter's Australian Open win in 1924 and his Victorian Amateur win in 1925 were both acclaimed victories. Like Whitton, Dalrymple and Russell were recognised as old campaigners.

Under their eminent golfer rule, Royal Melbourne also enfranchised good players without going through the standard but time-consuming processes of selection and interview of persons nominated for membership. C.H. (George) Fawcett, from Tasmania, who had been a casualty of mustard gas in World War I, teamed effectively with Alex Russell to win the prestigous *Australasian* Foursomes title six times in the 1920s. Sloan Morpeth, from New Zealand, also played at Royal Melbourne. In 1920, 1927 and 1929, he won the New Zealand Amateur Championship and in 1928, won the New Zealand Open. In 1929, he appeared on the Victorian scene and won the Victorian Amateur Championship. Subsquently, he became the secretary-manager at Commonwealth and influential in the organisation of golf in Australia and acted as referee at many major events over the decade. From 1930, he was secretary of the Australian Golf Union. He married Susie Tolhurst, a prominent player at Royal Melbourne.

The top level of amateur golf, the expansion in the popularity of sport and its consequences was not all happily received. David Worley in his biography, *Bill Edgar*, reports Edgar's recollections of Ivo Whitton and Syd Dalrymple at the final of the *Australasian* Foursomes Shield event in 1933 after they had defeated him and Fred Bulte. When shaking hands, Syd Dalrymple told them, *It was good that we won. I was glad to have beaten you little upstart bastards*. Harry had to learn to deal with the personal politics that operated within and between the golf clubs.

Because Harry was at the top of golf in Victoria, his interest in who was playing well now extended to professional players although their playing paths crossed only at annual Open tournaments organised by a number of clubs. George Naismith, born in 1909 and his cousin, Ted Naismith, born in 1911 were prominent in professional ranks. The cousins came from working class Richmond and learned to play golf along the Yarra. For them, golf was a source of cash and they looked to caddying to supplement their family's incomes - 1/3d a round after they gave the caddie master his threepence commission. Ted became the assistant professional at Royal Melbourne in the 1920s and George, the professional at Riversdale.

During the 1931 pennant season, competition was lively and Harry performed well. He worked at his golf and was to be seen out on the practice green putting and putting until his touch was sure. By the time of the state championships, Harry's play and practice over the previous two years was rewarded. With Ron Harris, Harry won the Victorian Amateur Foursomes Championship. At the end of the week, Harry further vindicated the confidence placed in him. He won the Victorian Amateur Championship.

Looking back on the event, Harry admitted to a degree of tension. He played Gus Jackson in the first round and said that when he stood on the first tee, *I could hardly hold my club for tembling with nervousness. On the very first green, when I went to address my ball – some 40 feet away from the pin – I absolutely shook with fright; but for some unaccountable reason, the ball responded to my nervous stroke and landed clean into the hole!* Harry continued, cutting through the poetic licence of reports of the incident, *It was a tremendous shock to me – and rather amusing, particularly when I read in the paper how I 'cooly sank a 40-foot putt'!* Harry's direct approach to the game was already clear. He concluded, *After the first hole, I warmed up to the task in hand.*

By the final, on Saturday, 8 August 1931, Harry had conquered his nerves. At the same time as Ted Theodore, the federal treasurer, was finally acquitted of charges of corruption on the national stage, Harry prepared to meet Mick Ryan at Victoria Golf Club in a different sort of trial. Eric and Doll with Dick Payne and his mother Edith, who was a friend of Doll's, were excited members of the gallery of about 1,000 people following the event. Before the game began, Eric said to a friend, *For goodness sake, look after the boy, I'm not going near him, I'll worry him.* Then he proceeded to follow the match and ride out every shot, following each drive anxiously, his whole body tense with concentration as the players putted. By the third hole, Doll was really anxious for Harry had won the first hole and lost the second, *I'll be glad when it's over. I think I'm more excited than he is*, she admitted to Edith Payne.

The final was over 36 holes. In the morning's round, Harry was outdriving Mick consistently - he took a four on the 576 yard 9th hole - but his putting was letting him down. They went into lunch with Mick leading. In the gallery, the word was that Ryan's maturity and cool head would see him pull away and win by a wide margin. Amounts of money were exchanged to this end.

Harry started the afternoon round well and, although he made a few mistakes, the putts began to drop and his accuracy with his irons to the green increased. At the 33rd hole, he was three up, but sliced his tee shot into the sand dunes on the left. Mick drove straight down the fairway and then approached well on to the green. It looked sure that Mick would win the hole and start his run. But from the sand, and having to stand very awkwardly, Harry selected a 7-iron and hit his ball so straight that it hit the pin and stopped dead. Harry always remembered this shot as one of his most fortuitous. As he admitted, he *wasn't feeling a bundle of confidence over the approach to this trapped green and that gave me the championship.* In the end, it was an easy win - four up with three to play.

When Harry won, Eric and Doll were much gratified by the praise heaped upon him. *He was so cool. He was so modest. No one had doubted it. His powers had been evident for several years now. Remember the Monthly Medal he had won when he was fourteen.* The trophy was imposing, given by the Right Honourable Lord Forster of Lepse, and the title, Victorian Amateur Champion, it was impressed on Harry, was one of the most coveted in the land. Harry, shy in public, blushed with the novelty of the occasion and managed to say a few words, thanking Mick Ryan for the game and his parents in particular.

As onlookers adjusted to Harry's youth, another aspect of his game attracted attention - he was left-handed. It was observed that Mick Ryan had narrowly defeated a left-hander - Len Nettlefold from Tasmania - the previous year to win the Victorian Amateur Championship and that, now, another left-hander had defeated him. Left-handers all around Victoria read the reports of his victory with delight. Only about 5% of Victorian golfers were left-handed and now they had a new champion. Years before, in 1909, when Claude Felstead won the Australian Open title at Royal Melbourne, so delighted were left-handers in Melbourne that they presented him with a purse of sovereigns. In 1931, such excesses of enthusiasm were blunted by the difficulties of a Depression but Harry gained a firm following from the left-handed fraternity.

This time the pictures in the newspapers had Harry in nearly every one of them. The *Age* and the *Argus* had less sport and fewer pictures but now Doll wanted them all. Eric would buy the *Herald* of an evening to read after his dinner and Doll bought the weekly *Table Talk* at the newsagents to read the social news of the day. Now, with Harry's success Doll bought everything, and as well, the *Sporting Globe* and the *Australasian* to relive Harry's successes. In the *Australasian* of 15 August 1931 there was a whole page of photographs. Harry putting. Harry driving on the fairway at the 16th. Harry playing out of the rough. Harry walking between tees. Doll spread the pages out at Queenie's and together with Eileen and Marie looked over them debating which of them was the best likeness. Harry treated all this with a smile but he continued to practice for the national events, only a week away in Sydney.

After his success in the Victorian Championships, the club selectors named Harry in the Victorian amateur team to play against New South Wales later in August. Doll bought Harry a new set of plus fours and he was photographed with the cream of Victorian golf. With him were Charlie Smith, Alex Russell, Henry Schlapp (all from Victoria) Ivo Whitton (Royal Melbourne), L.H. McPherson and Mick Ryan from Kingston Heath. The success of Victoria in the pennant season was reflected in the number of members from the Club represented in the photograph.

Eric and Doll made plans to take Harry to Sydney for the national championships starting in the middle of August 1931. Travelling interstate was a major undertaking and Doll bustled around in the days after the Amateur title, making arrangements for the trip to Sydney. She was delighted. She liked a holiday and to follow Harry around as part of the gallery was delightful, if nerve-wracking. Even if the New South Wales Savings Bank had closed its doors and the demagogue Jack Lang was a menace to decent Australia, Sydney was a pleasant destination.

Doll, Eric and Harry travelled by car, taking two or three days for the journey and stopping overnight at Albury and Wagga Wagga. It was Harry's first trip away from Melbourne and Doll and Eric made sure that everything went smoothly. They booked in at the Wentworth and, at Eric's insistence, as soon as they had unpacked, bathed and changed, walked down to see the recently completed span of the Sydney Harbour Bridge.

Although Harry was convinced that Melbourne was the home of golf in Australia - after all, Royal Melbourne had organised the first championship and it had been Royal Melbourne which had asked Royal Sydney and Royal Adelaide to form the Australian Golf Union - the championships in Sydney showed him that golf was played as well if not better there and that the game had also been played longer there.

As in Melbourne, there had been an expansion of golf from an early preserve of clubs established by the wealthy and influential men of the city. In 1882, members of the Union Club formalised their play on the Sydney Common, later Moore Park, and established the Australian Golf Club. When enthusiasm for playing there waned, members moved to land at Concord where the Sydney Golf Club was formed in 1893.

The original layout of the 9-hole golf course between Old South Head Road and the Pacific Ocean replicated as far as possible a traditional links course. In 1897, it was extended to 18-holes and, on opening the new clubhouse, the governor announced the right to the prefix 'Royal' had been granted by Queen Victoria. Meanwhile, members of the Australian Club revived the course at Kensington. These two courses - Royal Sydney and the Australian - were used for the Australian championships and Harry was eager to make their acquaintance.

Golf in New South Wales in 1931 had, as in Melbourne, benefited from its increased popularity during the previous decade. In 1920, there were sixty clubs affiliated to the N.S.W. Golf Council; by 1930, there were one hundred. Major investments expanded existing clubs. In 1923, an impressive Spanish hacienda style clubhouse was built at Manly and in 1926, the Australian course was renovated. New golf clubs were established. Public courses appeared. Moore Park, the best known, was formed in 1920 for golfers to play on the old Sydney Common and became an 18-hole course in 1923.

As in Melbourne, there was a circle of top players who met regularly in different combinations to play golf competitively. Like Melbourne, there were divisions between professionals and amateurs. Frank Eyre, the leading Australian professional of the period had established his career in 1926 when he won £500 prize money donated by the Sydney *Sun* for the winner of the Australian Professional championship. In 1930, he won the Australian Open. Eyre was also a keen surfer. Harry Sinclair was another who began his career as an amateur. He came from the working class suburb of Redfern and started playing at Moore Park where he worked as a caddie after school and then as greenkeeper. After winning the Australian Amateur Championship in 1926, he turned professional.

By contrast, in the amateur ranks were golfers like Eric Apperly, who won the Australian Amateur Championship in 1920, but was by now as well known as the architect of substantial club houses at numerous clubs including Manly and Killara. Then there was Harry Hattersley and Tom McKay, each of whom appeared the ideal amateur golfer. Hattersley, born in 1908, and McKay, born in 1909, were educated at Sydney Church of England Grammar School. Hattersley was an outstanding athlete, cricketer, rower and rugby player. On leaving school, he became a successful accountant and stockbroker. At golf, too, he was successful, winning the Australian Amateur championship in 1930. Neither a smoker nor a drinker, Harry Hattersley, in his plus fours and with upright demeanour was the epitome of a team man. Meanwhile, Tom McKay, the son of Claude McKay, the editor of *Smith's Weekly*, went on to study law at Sydney University and to captain the University golf team.

The debate over youth versus age also occupied the minds of golfers in Sydney. At the recent New South Wales titles of 1931, Dan Soutar's triumph in the state Professional championship at the age of sixty-nine brought satisfied comment from some. Gus Jackson reported a conversation he'd had with Dan Soutar during a period when he thought he has lost his nerve for championship golf. *I can still play the good stuff, Gus*, he said, *but these days when a big competition gets under way I tremble and shake as though the club in my hands were a 'death adder' about to bite me*. It was therefore, pleasing for golfers to read of his return to the winning list. But, on the other side, Jim Ferrier's success in winning the New South Wales Amateur title at only sixteen pushed the claims of youth with equal force.

Therefore, although the names were different and the weather was several degrees warmer, it was still golf. Harry appreciated his parents running round, finding out all the details of the tournament and organising his entries. The golf became mixed up with the comings and goings of a stay in Sydney and the company of golfers. Doll and Eric became friendly with others in the gallery. In particular, Doll found the golf writers congenial and, as some were staying at the same hotel, they discussed the unfolding drama of the days with interest. Jack Dillon was good company and he and his wife, Eva, often joined them at dinner.

Doll liked the novelty of Sydney. She might have seen people loitering in the Domain or sitting in Hyde Park, but they were part of a reality that existed outside her experience. There were Williams relatives in Sydney so there were arrangements to meet up with aunts and cousins living in the comfortable suburbs around the harbour. At night, Doll and Eric might go to Gladys Moncrieff at the Capitol and there was always the pictures - Ramon Novarro's playing his Most Romantic role in 'Son of India' at the Plaza or the more thrilling 'Dirigible', soaring into New and Wondrous Realms at the Lyceum. But primarily the whole family was absorbed by the day to day events of the tournament.

8

In Sydney, in August 1931, the hopes and dreams that Doll and Eric held for their son all appeared to be realised. Here Harry was hailed, at the age of sixteen, as a brilliant golfer and ready to perform on the national stage. Indeed, the reception of Harry Williams threatened to take on a life of its own, independent of his own inclinations in the matter.

The appearance of two sixteen year old boys - Harry Williams and Jim Ferrier - vying for national honours was a matter of great excitement. Ivo Whitton had burst on to the scene as a youth. But here were two at the one time. The press clustered around them as stars who would carry messages of youthful achievement into every home in the nation. And most apt, they could be seen to represent Sydney and Melbourne rivalries.

Harry and Jim were acclaimed as celebrities. The front pages of the newspapers carried stories with headlines announcing them as 'Boy Wonders' or 'Wonder Boys'. It was a Youth's Invasion cried Jack Dillon in the *Sporting Globe*. He drew on biblical allusions to make his point, *While some are attempting to explain that golf is an old man's game, Davids in their early 'teens are tearing from the heads of former Goliaths of the links State and other crowns*. He continued, *I realise that as golfers they are little short of prodigies* and, indeed, their achievements on the golf course were significant.

But also of significance was that the two boys were from the amateur ranks. They were not playing golf to earn a living but because of the love of the game. Around them coalesced the convictions of a sporting culture that idealised the playing of sport without overt commercial trappings.

Table Talk and the *Bulletin* carried columns on golf for the socially aware reader. There, it was assumed that golf was club golf, a sport for and by amateurs. Moreover, as Harry and Jim were respective state amateur champions, they were equally credentialled. 1931 was to be the year in which the young guns announced their presence at the top of Australian golf.

A match between the two sixteen-year-old golfers was arranged with the proceeds to go to charity. At first, three matches, under the auspices of the *Referee*, were proposed but this was reduced to one that would take place before the championships began.

The 13 August 1931 edition of *Table Talk* elevated news of the proposed match between Harry Williams and Jim Ferrier to their pages, Table Talk of the Week, devoted to The Latest Topics, People in the News and What People Are Saying And Doing. The proposed match was news along with paragraphs announcing, Spring is Coming and the arrival of The New Consul for China. Apart from the topical, there were paragraphs on A Solid Rock, which proved to be the Australian Mutual Provident Society, information on India and Skulls - Anthropology and comment that a Labor Ministry in Britain *is no good for us*. A new portrait of the Queen of Roumania gave the page a patrician gloss.

Amateur golf fitted into this world as a significant activity. It was important news. It also embellished the idea of Harry and Jim as exceptional, leading with the statement that *quite a sensation in the world occurred this week when 16-year-old Harry Williams won the Amateur Championship of Victoria*. The meat of the paragraph came at the end when the reader learned that, *Curiously enough, the N.S.W. champion is also a lad of sixteen.* Like racehorses, *it is hoped to match these two youthful champions at an early date'* and the paragraph concluded, *It should certainly be a match worth seeing.*

There were some reservations. Gus Jackson, who played at Kingston Heath and who wrote the weekly golf column in *Table Talk* wrote in the 20 August 1931 edition with concern that the contest between Harry and Jim was assuming unseemly proportions. After discussing the relative merits of the field for the forthcoming championships, Gus Jackson warned Harry's admirers, *Stand clear of this boy and give him breathing space. He has the quality of golf and courage that wins without any urging from admirers. Already*, Jackson thought, *the hot air valve has been opened too wide regarding his proposed match against Jim Ferrier, which is not going to do the play of these lads any good.*

Jackson did not see any problem with Ferrier and Harry playing a match. *The public is anxious that these players should meet, and the lads themselves have no objections to a match.* But he did object to the followers who would look, not at the skills of the two protagonists but for material to fuel their prejudices. *One has been thrown at the other by groups of plus four toggery who will find fault with the play, even although there may be no fault to find.* Jackson concluded cryptically, *Butchered to make a golfing holiday is a fitting expression to the proposed Ferrier-Williams match.*

With these misgivings aside, on Friday 22 August, the press and the public were given the opportunity to view two youthful prodigies in action. Doll and Eric oversaw Harry's days, sending him off to bed and talking on into the night with other members of the golfing fraternity staying at the hotel, basking in the reflected admiration. On the Friday, Eric took Harry out to Royal Sydney at Rose Bay for a morning round. When Doll caught up with them at lunch, she was pleased to find Harry in a cheerful mood for he had completed the eighteen in 73 and had gained some impression of the different holes on the course.

In the afternoon, Jim Ferrier arrived and, although both boys were assured that this was a friendly match both recognised that, already, they were in a state of rivalry. Jim Ferrier came from a golfing family. His grandfather had played at Carnoustie in Scotland but had gone to China to establish a golf course for British expatriates at Shanghai in the nineteenth century. Jim's father began playing golf in China before he came to Sydney where he became secretary at Manly Golf Club. Young Jim, born in 1915, was sent off to Sydney Grammar School where he played rugby until a knee injury forced him off the field and to the golf course. Jim now worked in the city but played golf every opportunity he had. He had an unorthodox swing - to protect his knee, he dipped his shoulder as he swung - but because of his strength, Jim still hit a very long ball.

Harry felt rather like a boxer with his seconds as Jim was introduced to him. The *Referee* introduced the two to its readers as opposites:
The Rapier. Williams. Lean, lithesome, loose-limbed. Small clear-cut features, dark curly hair. Eyes, jaw and a mouth of a fighter. Radiates nervy energy. Palmolive complexion plus Pullover, plus-fours, stocking and shoes - all brown.
The Sabre. Ferrier. Big, heavy of shoulder and limbs. Looks his fourteen stone. Full, round face. Roses and cream complexion. Blond in excelsis. Fair hair, suavely greased and parted. Lumbering, powerful, phlegmatic. More colourfully dressed with soft collar and tie.
To the crowd, they were perfect protagonists with two different styles of golf as well - Harry with an easy orthodox movement as compared to Jim's more awkward swing. Their youth stimulated the crowd. They might be looking at champions who would go on to challenge British golfers on their home turf. They were heady with the contemplation of such possibilities.

Even though there had been little publicity outside the regular golf columns in the newspapers, a gallery had gathered at Rose Bay. By now, both Harry and Jim were familiar with galleries but this was different for it had come together to watch them specifically. It was a large shifting crowd of 3,000 people, constantly moving to gain vantage points from which to view the two golfers, and expressing, as if one, sighs of disappointment or cries of elation. Once on the first fairway, however, both Harry and Jim settled into the familiar rhythms of the game.

The match was very even. At one stage, Harry was two up but Jim battled doggedly, winning the next two and putting himself back into contention. The game was won on the 18th. On this last hole, Jim was already on the green expecting to win it for Harry had strayed into a deep bunker. Instead, Harry produced a superb shot out of the bunker, made his putt, which gave him a half and the game. The play of the tiger prevailed. The model of Walter Hagen was also strong. According to Back Spin in the *Referee*, Harry *was a replica of Walter Hagen, whose face in the course of a big match is an inscrutable as that of the sphinx of the Pyramids*. He had learned his lessons well.

Although the Williams-Ferrier match had been billed as the first opportunity for a sporting public to witness a contest between the two best sixteen-year-olds in Australia, golf writers were careful to couch it in appropriate terms of golfing etiquette. *They're a pair of bonny boys*, an onlooker commented as Eric shook Harry's hand and Jim saluted his mother with a big kiss. It was observed that Ferrier smiled cheerfully when Williams won and that *the boys are firm friends*. Given that they had only met that afternoon, this observation was a little premature but deferred to the amateur ethos of the sport. The winner collected tickets - 6/- for the Dress Circle - to 'The Gondoliers', into its last days at the Theatre Royal and Harry, in a sporting gesture, took Jim as part of the party. In the morning's paper, the two youths - *friendly rivals* - were thought sufficiently newsworthy to be billed as opposition to the stage show and were entitled, Attractions In The Box. So ended the prelude.

There was a brief interruption to the Williams-Ferrier contest. On Saturday, Harry was invited with the rest of the golfers visiting Sydney to play in The Australian Club's stroke handicap event. It was quite leisurely, with both a morning and an afternoon field. Harry was pleased he was drawn in the afternoon when the chilly westerly had died down and he turned in a 79. He had played well but had found it difficult to judge the greens and had three putted at least four. Jim Ferrier played in the morning and had the best scratch card of the day, *a faultless 74*. But, now that he was working, Jim wanted additional practice. As soon as he finished his round, he left for Manly to play in the weekly club competition. He turned in the best scratch score there too with a card of 79.

Harry and his parents had a quiet day on the Sunday. Harry had a couple of boils on his neck that Doll bathed and dressed regularly. In the afternoon, they took a steamer ride around the harbour from Circular Quay to view the Bridge from different angles. Then, when they got back to the hotel, Harry and Eric got out the *Sydney Mail* that was running Secrets of Good Golf by Bobby Jones and studied the photographs closely. Then, it was an early night for Harry.

9

The very words, the Australian Open Championship and the Australian Amateur Championship of 1931, filled Harry, Doll and Eric with a thrill of anticipation. They looked at the tee off times for the Open. The name H. L. Williams was on the sheet. He had arrived. Not only that, the name of Harry Williams was on everyone's lips as a likely possibility to win the event. They counted down the days and then the hours till it would start.

During the 1920s, the Championships lost their earlier appearance of a series of pleasant games sandwiched between longer periods of hospitality. They brought together golfers from the eastern States but Victoria and New South Wales were most strongly represented. There were also players from Queensland, Tasmania and South Australia, but the issue of distance impeded truly national events. It was only in December of 1930 that Western Australia had been linked to the east by phone.

The Australian championships extended over more than a week. Golfers without adequate finances or in work they were unable to leave, therefore found it difficult to attend. Unless possible winners, professionals were unwilling to forego earnings for the period demanded. There was an increasing number of calls to separate the events, as the competition side of the championships increased, the demands of playing the Open followed by the Amateur and Professional Championships placed heavier pressures on the players. However, the efficiency of bringing all golfers together once only prevailed.

Harry now met golfers from the other states. Len Nettlefold, another left-hander from Tasmania, had won the Australian Amateur title in 1926 and 1928. Coming from a wealthy background due to extensive pastoral

72

and business interests, Len's occupation as a car and tractor salesman for his father's business in Hobart did not interfere with his lifestyle. He was considered something of a playboy on the golfing scene for his opportunities to travel and play golf were plentiful. He spent 1927 in Britain and competed in the British Open at St Andrews with success; his first round of 71 was a record. Back in Australia and playing at Royal Sydney in the Amateur Championship in 1928, on the 29th hole when he was being well beaten, his father, Robert, promised him his Buick if he won. Len duly drove off in the Buick.

On Monday, the Amateur Foursomes title opened the 1931 Championships at the Australian Club at Kensington. For Harry, it provided an enjoyable diversion. Harry was paired with the veteran Alex Russell and opened with a costly 82 in the morning although they retrieved themselves in the afternoon with a 76. Sloan Morpeth and Mick Ryan found trouble on the greens, which were very fast and puzzled all the interstate golfers. The Royal Sydney pair, George Fawcett, now in Sydney, and Reg Bettington, won the event. Eric Apperley partnered by Jim Ferrier came in second.

The next day, Tuesday 25 August, the interstate match was played and another round in the Williams-Ferrier contest created more than usual public interest in the event. Victoria played New South Wales in the morning and of course, the meeting of Ferrier and Williams was a feature. The weather was beautiful and a large gallery again followed the play. As with their first meeting, Harry established a lead but Jim worked hard to push the contest to the last hole, Harry winning at the 19th. The greens were fast and bumpy. Jim kept overhitting his approaches while Harry's chipping was deadly and indeed, on one green he holed a shot from a bunker. In the other matches, Ivo Whitton and Mick Ryan had both won and Charlie Smith had lost. The Victorians then played the Queensland team that had beaten South Australia in the other morning match. Ivo Whitton and Mick Ryan lost, surprisingly, and Queensland won the day.

As the Championships loomed, the relative merits of Jim Ferrier and Harry Williams took on wider currency. A contest such as this was good copy for the sporting press, appealing to a wider readership than just members of the major golf clubs. The appearance of Ferrier and Williams at the top of amateur ranks spilled into the popular interest in golf. Jack Dillon, a prominent golf writer whose work mainly appeared in the *Sporting Globe* observed that *while the championship games are on, golf is discussed in field, shop and office, and the chances of boy and man, amateur or professional, are as animatedly discussed as is football on a Saturday night*. Columns in the dailies and in sporting newspapers before the major events became guides to the form of players for betting on the outcome of the events.

For a fortnight each year, golf moved beyond the confines of state boundaries to assume national sporting significance. Good scores from professional as well as amateur ranks were advanced as evidence of the standard of golf in Australia. The Australian Open and the accompanying championships provided rankings of the best golfers in the country and assured the events of wide public attention.

On the Wednesday evening, the night before the Open began, talk centred on who would win. Journalists, Jack Dillon and Gus Jackson debated the issue. Gus opened the conversation.
I would have said that Ivo Whitton was a certainty, but Bill Boyce beat him comfortably on Monday in the interstate match. I don't think that Ivo is as good a match player as he once was. Perhaps he could do better in the Open.
Jack Dillon nodded,
Hattersley would be a likely possibility but he's been concentrating on his accountancy work. George Fawcett is playing steady golf but he's probably getting a bit old to stand the pace now.
I don't know, Gus interjected, *although you wouldn't call him brilliant,*

74

he's very accurate with his wood and iron shots and that's the sort of play that wears down the opponent. And, steadiness matters in the Open because it is a real test of concentration. This is why I don't think Williams and Ferrier will win.

Gus looked at Jack Dillon for denial for those two golfers were figuring largely in the betting for the event. Gus continued,

From watching Williams, he can certainly play golf, but, in my view, all this attention is like a load of lead on his shoulders. Everyone is giving him advice. He'd be better off if they all left him alone. Jim Ferrier is lucky he's in home territory but the fanfare for every game Williams plays is too distracting.

Yes, I realise that as golfers they are little short of prodigies. Williams can hit a golf ball better and more truly, and keep it up longer, than any player I have seen this year. Probably Ferrier can do the same thing. Still, I don't think either of the lads is capable of winning an Open yet. I don't think they'll go the journey.

Jack persisted.

It's not because of the attention they're getting, I don't think. They both appear to be able to concentrate on their golf when they're playing. No, it's more the type of golf the Open demands. When they won their State titles, they had to concentrate on getting into the first sixteen places to qualify for the match play. Qualifying through the stroke rounds didn't really cause them that much trouble because both of them are good golfers. Then they had to win four matches. In those matches, their task was each day to play better golf than the man who was the immediate opponent. If he played only moderately well, all they had to do was to be a little better. By being better on each day than the opponent for four consecutive days, they won through.

Jack warmed to the subject.

Boys are not built with the stamina or personality to stand four rounds of stroke play without the strain getting to them. You can't

belt a golf ball over twenty miles through a series of fixed hazards without having a lapse at some point. Then, it starts to eat into them that someone else is getting an advantage and that affects their shot-making if they're not careful. They're not built to stand that kind of thing and, at the same time, give of their best.

Given that, said Gus, *if you were to pick a winner from them, which would you pick?*

Jack considered the question carefully and responded:

The fact that Williams won the match he played against Ferrier on Friday by a single hole is not sufficiently significant to indicate who is the better player. However, the Victorian lad was playing under the disadvantage of strange links, and after travelling up from Melbourne. In the foursomes on Monday, though, Ferrier's work was much better than Williams. By the time this is over, we'll have a much better idea of their relative abilities. What do you think?

Williams is a left-hander so that is normally considered a limitation. I remember Len Nettleton telling me that when he went to England in 1927, he said to the great man, H.J. Taylor that he was a left hander, Taylor held up his hands in horror. He thought he was wasting his money coming 10,000 miles and as a left-hander hoping to make a decent show in the British Open.

Jack Dillon laughed and named several left-handers who had been successful. Gus returned the conversation to the field for the Open.

What about amongst the pros? he asked, *Any of them a chance?*

Well, the Victorian team finished last in the interstate match although Teddy Naismith could surprise. He has a really sweet swing and is one of the most promising players around. But then he has a passion for hooking and, like Ferrier and Williams, I don't know if he is hardened to the demands of the Open either.

That won't be a problem for Billy Bolger. He seems to have the big occasion temperament. He's got a powerful swing and he appears to be near enough to imperturbable. Then there's Charlie Gray, who is back from America and Joe Cohen - they were brilliant as boys at Moore Park. They could get up.

And so saying, Jack concluded the discussion by reminding Gus that he had a story to file for the *Sporting Globe* on the prospects of the field and he had better go and write it.

The first round of the Open took place on Thursday 27 August at the Australian Club, Kensington. The morning was lovely but by the early afternoon the wind had blown up so those who teed off later played with a strong westerly. After the second round on the Friday, Harry Williams was second, Ivo Whitton fourth and Jim Ferrier, twenty-seventh. Jim Ferrier completed a brilliant third round that rocketed him up through the list to be two strokes from Harry Williams. Harry now led the field with Ivo Whitton third, five strokes behind Ferrier.

The final round was gripping. Ivo Whitton staged a great comeback and news that he had completed the first nine in 33 travelled like wildfire around the course. The leaders faltered. Jim Ferrier took 40 to the turn and Harry with a disastrous seven at the 6th hole and four putts on two greens ended up taking an 80 for the round. The Open became a contest between Whitton and Ferrier. On the last hole, Jim Ferrier drove well, needing a five to tie. But he pushed his second shot wide and ended up taking a six.

Ivo Whitton, the veteran, won the title. Ivo, however, had lost his favourite felt hat he always wore when playing golf and appeared more concerned about that than his victory. Nevertheless, when he accepted the trophy, Whitton, a polished public speaker, made sure that he paid tribute to the great performances of the two boys, Ferrier and Williams. Both played magnificently, he concluded and, in his opinion, young Ferrier was unlucky to lose. The patron of the Australian Club, Sir John Vicars, echoed the remarks. After congratulating Ivo Whitton on winning the event in sporting style, he referred in glowing terms to the doings of these magnificent colts, Ferrier and Williams. Their game was the greatest he had seen for years and he thanked them for it.

All interest now turned to the national Amateur title as the first five places in the Open had been filled by amateurs, promising a strong contest. Harry was beginning to feel the pace. The boils on his neck were still painful. But on the Sunday night, Harry appreciated a brief interlude in his schedule. The tournament organisers arranged a private screening for the visitors of four of the newly arrived Bobby Locke Remarkable Sound Film Series, 'How I Play Golf' which Harry attended with interest. But then he couldn't sleep. At 2 a.m., when Doll saw Harry's bedroom light still on and went in, she found him sitting up dealing out bridge hands. So she had called the kitchen for a hot drink to be brought up with a sandwich and then sat with him till he fell asleep.

On the Monday Harry defeated George Fawcett five and four and on Tuesday, Tom McKay four and three. In the semi-finals on Wednesday he met Ferrier. At the end of the mornings round, Harry was leading and Jim, not happy with his form, following a hasty lunch was out on the course practising on the putting green and straightening out his drive. Harry, however, continued in the groove and won comfortably. When shaking hands, Harry, rather timidly, asked Jim if he'd like some cakes or an ice-cream but Ferrier just looked away and walked to the putting green for more practice. Next day in the final, Harry beat George Thompson three and two.

When Harry Williams won the Australian Amateur title in 1931, his name joined an illustrious list of previous winners already engraved on the trophy. George Thompson, the runner-up, in his speech very sportingly admitted that he had enjoyed every minute of the game and never wanted to meet a better opponent. Eric and Doll were overjoyed and repaired to the clubhouse to celebrate. When they looked for Harry several hours later, they found him asleep in their car, parked around the back in a shelter shed, a half-eaten package of Sultana Luncheons on the seat beside him.

Winning the title was symbolic of his rite of passage from a youthful prodigy to the holder of the national amateur title. It entered Harry's name in the holy books of the sport. At the time, Harry's application for membership at Victoria Golf Club had already been rejected once and was before the committee again. It was timely that Jack Dillon, as the only Victorian journalist at the titles, should devote his column in *The Sporting Globe* to assuring Melbourne readers that Harry was a suitable occupant of the amateur throne.

Dillon admitted that stories had been told that Harry had, as a young boy, somewhat of a temper, and formerly was alleged to have given it a piece of rein on the links. This gossip, Dillon proposed, was untrue, unkind and too harsh on a youngster. Harry was, after all, *a human Australian boy*. Indeed, Jack Dillon reported, in Sydney Harry was *the complete little gentleman*. Others concurred. Captain Walker, secretary of the Australian Golf Club found Harry *a thoroughly admirable type of Australian boy*. Rather than opposing Harry's membership, it was congratulations to Victoria Golf Club on the gaining the most promising piece of talent yet found in Australia.

In the wash-up of the tournament, the deeds of Harry Williams and Jim Ferrier preoccupied the pundits. They had played three games. Each contest had been close. The armchair experts clutched at clues to guide their predictions. It was observed that throughout their match play contests, Ferrier had never once managed to get ahead of Harry. Certainly, on the evidence of the 1931 Championship titles, Harry Williams was the star of the year.

With these three matches, Harry Williams and Jim Ferrier were locked into a state of rivalry in the mind of the golfing public. The reports of the matches described two different approaches to the game. Harry appeared the more expert maker of shots, more golfer-like and there were criticisms of Ferrier's grip. Harry, it was said, *is much more of an artist than the Manly youth, and his long swinging drives and beautifully played irons were a delight to the connoisseur*. By contrast, Ferrier, *is by no means a stylist, but his short game and his courage have been his outstanding characteristics*.

Of all the golfers Harry was to meet, it was perhaps only Jim who Harry believed he could defeat whenever they met. Harry was critical of Jim's style, and considered that he possessed better skills. Certainly, Jim looked at times a very ordinary player on the fairways but in putting he excelled. Harry tended to dismiss putting as primarily a matter of practice and remained confident that superior golf must prevail. At the time, Harry thought Jim's nickname, The Wolf, coined it was said for his ability to scare his opponents, was not likely to challenge successfully the grace and strength of The Tiger on the course.

The Williams family returned to Melbourne well pleased with themselves. There was quite a welcoming party for them at Wellington Street when they arrived back. Dick told Harry that the boys at Brighton Grammar had organised a golf day at the old Royal Melbourne links the Thursday he played in the Amateur title to mark his national success. In the succeeding days of their homecoming, reporters beat a path to the Williams's home in Wellington Street to pose Harry with the cup and family dog for the Melbourne newspapers. Harry Williams was a star.

10

Early in 1932, the Williams family moved from Brighton to take up residence at 68 Milton Street, St Kilda or as it was increasingly known Elwood. The house was on a corner block in 'Poet's Corner' where the names of English literary greats conferred on the streets an intellectual air. Some lead lighting added a decorative touch to the red brick Edwardian house with its small formal front garden and a yard at the back where Harry could practise his chipping. The grid pattern of the streets was still fairly bare. As there were only a few motor cars, the streets were largely left to the various hawkers, deliverymen and the children.

The move was seen as advantageous. The new house was close to Queenie's and Doll welcomed this. It was also part of Eric's plans for the family's future. Eric had finally found a business that suited him and offered an occupation for Harry. He bought a newsagency at 207 Barkly Street, St Kilda, which included a circulating library and the rights to sell newspapers from a kiosk at the St Kilda railway station. Eric also joined himself and Harry as members at the Sandridge Golf Club, which maintained golf on the old Victoria Golf Club site at Fisherman's Bend.

The newsagency was in a good position, in the shopping strip that was really a continuation of busy Acland Street. It nestled in a cluster of shops that served east St Kilda and north Elwood and stretched along both sides of Barkly Street at the junction with Acland Street. It catered for a suburban clientele. There were a couple of grocers, butchers and confectioners and a scattering of pastrycook, cakeshop, fishmonger and fruiterer. For general household needs, there were two chemists, an ironmonger, a decorator, a Chinese laundry and a dry cleaner. Attending to the person required a range of shops: a mercer, milliner, dressmaker, watchmaker and jeweller, boot repairer, two hairdressers, and a sports goods and tailor shop. Social life, however, was limited to the Village Belle hotel and dining rooms that were shut by 7 p.m. W. Dickinson's Antique Shop, more correctly a second hand market, an estate agent and a bank completed the array. In the inner city suburbs, wine saloons, pawnbrokers and fish and chip shops showed different domestic patterns but here in East St Kilda, retail served a comfortable but thrifty residential population.

Sixteen-year-old Harry, after the successes of the previous year, was hazy about his future. When questioned, Harry anticipated making a trip abroad to play golf when he was about twenty but expected to have some career by then. Eric had definite ideas. He expected Harry to assist him in the business and, in particular, to take responsibility for selling newspapers from the kiosk at the railway station. Harry's reputation, Eric thought, would be used to advantage there. Harry found the demands of the job tiresome for they disrupted the agreeeable habits to which he had grown accustomed and which, by 1932, were very well established.

By 1932, the Depression was biting deeper into the structures of the society. In December 1931, Joe Lyons had swept into government in a landslide but the effects of financial dislocation increased. Registered unemployment of members of trade unions in Australia reached 30%. Even in the cosy homes of the members of golf clubs, financial pressures pushed domestic economies to the limit. In July, the directors of the Victoria Golf Club accepted the resignations of thirty-two members and the financial restrictions undertaken the previous year remained in place.

If Harry thought about it, he was aware of more men as a physical presence on the streets. Sometimes he saw queues waiting in a line for food or work and gangs of men on sustenance were employed on building the Yarra Boulevard and the Shrine of Remembrance. Eric came home every day with stories of men coming in to the newsagency to ask whether he wanted to put on an extra hand. He pointed this out to Harry when they were arguing about Harry's work in the newsagency. But, if Harry gave a thought to the news of the day, it was to Walter Lindrum's world record break in billiards or, in April, the death of Phar Lap in the United States.

Generally, Harry's main interest was in upholding his position as the Victorian and Australian Amateur Champion. In the process, he found that he acquired the status of a young man rather than a boy. At Victoria Golf Club, too, Harry had earned his place. Although he was evidently playing well in 1931, he had not been selected to play in the *Australasian* Foursomes Shield that year. Now, following his national success, he and Gus Jackson carried off the Shield in 1932. Harry was no longer a student of the game. He had arrived. His golfing style was now taken as a model. But he was still only young. In December 1931, Harry was the subject of a long interview in *Golf*. As a teenager, starting out on a golfing career, he was presented as quiet and modest, as someone who only became enthusiastic and talkative when expressing his views about the thing he knew best, golf.

As a sixteen-year-old, Harry was more spoken about than spoken to. Eric, for instance, spoke for him. The *Referee* carried a letter received from Mr E. L. Williams, Middle Brighton (Vic) that attempted the definitive explanation of Harry's swing following the *notes and articles re my son's swing and the comments thereon*. He has the same swing as Bobby Jones, asserted Eric, and he referred to advice received from the professionals John Young and Alan Maiden in 1929 to leave Harry's natural inside out movement alone.

In July 1932, Harry turned seventeen and he began to be more closely watched for indications of his mature personality. Playing golf, of all sports, it was thought, most tellingly expressed the individual's character. In May, at the Open tournament held at Commonwealth, Harry and Bill Edgar's match drew a crowd of over 2,000, a bigger gallery than had turned out for the Hagen-Kirkwood exhibition matches. Harry, with calm and capable play, won the game. There were some downs. In the first round of the Club Championship at Victoria later in May where Harry now played, the contest narrowed to Harry and Gus Jackson. Ever the tiger, on the 12th, instead of going for safety, Harry attempted a risky shot that ended up costing him three strokes and the championship.

Over the next eight weeks, however, Harry's golf was disappointing. Harry put his losses down to lack of practice because of having to work at the newsagency. Harry argued that it stopped him playing golf as he wished. He sulked. In this attitude, Harry was strongly supported by Doll who, with a well-developed sense of privilege, sided with Harry in the view that golf was a sufficient vocation. She saw no reason for the best golfer in Australia to work for his living by selling newspapers at a railway station. Eric relented and Harry devoted himself to systematic practice.

At the end of July, Harry turned on a devastating exhibition in his pennant game against Metropolitan. On the first nine, Harry hacked his way around the course, looking like a novice. His opponent, Tom Graham was playing well and by the turn was five up. Then Harry's swing settled into a groove, his approaches became spot on, his putting precise - he'd had three putts on two greens and four putts on another in the first nine. At the 16th, Harry was still three down. All Graham had to do was to halve one of the remaining three holes. He continued to play steady golf and parred the three. But Harry covered himself with glory. He birdied the last three holes. The 16th - 474 yards in four, the 17th - 464 yards in

84

four, and the 18th - 430 yards in three to square the match. Then Harry won the 19th. Even after a few drinks, Tom Graham still shook his head in disbelief at the awesome display.

The brilliance of Harry's displays of golf intrigued onlookers. It was difficult to evaluate players. How good was Harry? In the *Sporting Globe*, Jack Dillon compared Harry with Joe Kirkwood. He argued that courses were more difficult than in 1920, when Kirkwood was setting records but that Harry was breaking 70 constantly. Twice in practice he had gone round Victoria in 65 and as well, despite his handicap of plus three, he was still amongst the regular winners in the weekly competition. On the Saturday before the article was written, for instance, he'd had 68 and missed winning the club handicap trophy by a stroke, a fourteen marker had a net 70.

But golf was also seen as a field of combat and if Harry was to be accepted into the ranks of the adult male golfers, showing a competitive character was essential. During the 1920s and early 1930s, as the standard of amateur golf improved so too did the call for more competition and, especially, the use of match play to accentuate golfers as rivals. Although golfers played to the par of the course and, ostensibly, played against the course, golf was also organised as a competitive sport between players. Harry's successes clearly defined him as the best golfer in Australia. He could play brilliant golf. But was he a tough competitor? Golf was such an individual sport that the usual keys of performance used in team sports such as loyalty and physical courage were not valid.

Contemporaries watched every word and action to find clues to the question. Each time Harry played, his performance was grist for the mill of sporting myth. In the final pennant match of the 1932 season, Victoria played Kingston Heath. Harry was drawn to play against Mick Ryan, which Mick won. Mick Ryan was playing well and later that month he won the Australian Open at Royal Adelaide and on his return, the Victorian Amateur Championship. But, in discussing the game, some argued that Harry lacked obstinacy, that he resigned the 6th hole and later the 12th hole well before they were irretrievably lost. Mick Ryan, a former champion in the team sports of football and cricket was seen to seize on Harry's resignation as a psychological boost to his play.

Criticisms that Harry was not a fighter were strong for they arose from a view of sport as building character through competition. But to Harry the opposition often appeared to mean little. By taking on the course as a tiger, as someone who enjoyed making his shots, Harry rejected the combative approach of playing the opposition. He had the confidence in his golf to play well and to take on anyone in the process. To some, though, his boldness was assumed to be merely a phase of youthful confidence that would pass and he would lose his accuracy to the greens.

Had Harry been a broad shouldered, extrovert American professional, his approach would have been seen as fitting his appearance. But as a fairly shy adolescent - he was described by one journalist as *comparatively frail looking* - this bold philosophy appeared to fit neither his personality nor his body shape. He was enjoined to take the orthodox path to manhood by showing grit and determination in the more conventional ways.

The Australian championships held in Adelaide in 1932 was the next major occasion when Harry's mettle was tried. After Melbourne, Adelaide was quiet. South Australia's economy had been first affected by the Depression and, in many aspects, was hardest hit. The number of unemployed was large and by the end of 1932, Adelaide had the worst unemployment of all national capitals. The effects, however, were largely unseen by Doll and Harry.

Harry and Doll travelled over by train and were house guests of members of Royal Adelaide. There was a busy round of functions arranged for the visitors - bridge parties, a dance at the Kooyonga clubhouse as well as several dinners. When she was shopping, Doll found the streets more subdued than in Melbourne but the main shopping area with their Department stores like John Martins, Moores and Myer's were reassuring. At the social events, people preferred to talk about the 'Bodyline' cricket test of the previous January than the extent of unemployment.

South Australia had its own prominent players. There was Rufus Stewart, professional at Kooyonga, who was regarded as one of the best professional golfers of the period and had won the 1927 Australian Open and was runner-up in 1926 and 1928.

Amongst the amateurs, Legh Winser, was a regular entrant in the national championships. Born in 1884, he had emigrated to South Australia from England in 1909 for a healthier climate, and became secretary to six successive Governors of South Australia. Winser had played first class cricket in England and so arrived with impressive sporting credentials which, when turned to golf, won him the Australian Amateur title in 1921.

Harry found the Royal Adelaide course a challenge. Royal Adelaide had opened at Seaton in 1907, on land developed as a links course like St Andrew's. In 1923, the club received the right to prefix 'Royal' to its title and three years later, Dr Alister Mackenzie, on his visit to Australia was invited to redesign the course to make it more suitable for championship play. By 1932, although the changes had lost their rawness, the course was considered the most difficult of those on which the Open was played. The holes that were laid out among sand dunes and hollows bristled with fearsome spiky tussocks and rushes.

Harry's presence at the championships created news. He was still presented as a boy thrust into centre stage by his precocious talent. His looks were described – *fresh complexioned, tall, and not yet by any means overgrown for his age*. His swing was studied – *a long, free backswing and tremendous pivot unwinds at terrific speed, and the wrists come through with a decided flick*. When pictures of the golfers for the papers were taken, Harry was drawn into the circle to be photographed. The old lions – Ivo Whitton and Arthur Le Fevre – reclined at the front of the pack with Harry tucked into the group at the back, an eager young cub. When the Australian Open finished on 19 August, Harry was sixth with an aggregate of 301, only five shots behind Mick Ryan's winning score.

Then Harry's defence of the Amateur title commenced. Harry's notoriety brought out the crowds. The gallery for the final of the Australian Amateur championship on Thursday 26 August trebled after lunch and men and women ran to secure vantage points around the green. Amongst the gallery of 4,000 was the Governor of South Australia who earlier in the year had captured the headlines with a hole-in-one. To the crowd, the Amateur title was represented as a contest between the older burly Dr Reg Bettington, known as Tarzan to the caddies at Royal Sydney, and the slender youthfulness of Harry Williams. Harry was two up at lunch and continued playing well in the afternoon. Bettington persisted and, drawing on his competitive talents, including setting a stymie for Harry at the 33rd, he won the title.

Bettington's victory pleased conventional wisdom that character, learned on the playing fields of school and university, was a crucial ingredient in golfing success. Reg Bettington was an ear, nose and throat specialist, born in 1900 and a schoolboy hero of King's School, Sydney. He had completed his education at Oxford, where he won blues in cricket, rugby and golf. On his return to Sydney, Bettington captained the NSW

Sheffield team and even trialled for the Test team. Both golfers had played well and, in golfing circles it was considered one of the most exciting finals of the title. But tenacity won the day.

Governor Sir Alexander Hore-Ruthven had consoling words for Doll, when he congratulated her on Harry's fine golf and his fine sportsmanship. *I would advise you,* he said, *to send Harry to Britain if that is possible. I am sure he would do well in big golf there.* Doll was much impressed by the Governor's conversation with her and on her return, relayed it word for word and gesture for gesture to successive audiences. On his return from Seaton, Harry was unexpectedly defeated in the early rounds of the Victorian Amateur championship and Mick Ryan, continuing his winning streak, took out the title. But Harry returned to the winner's circle in the new year. On the 1933 Australia Day weekend, Harry won the Sorrento Open for the third time.

By the beginning of 1933, the seventeen-year-old Harry had developed a reputation for a laconic nonchalance. This attitude was at odds with prevailing ideas of the successful golfer as a model of vigorous determination. The 1933 Sorrento tournament added another anecdote to the myth. Dick Payne picked Harry up to travel down to Sorrento. When they reached Frankston and were talking over Harry's success in the event in the previous years, Dick looked over to the back seat where Harry had flung his coat. *Have you brought the trophy?* he asked. Harry looked surprised, *Trophy, what trophy?* he queried. Dick explained. *It's a perpetual trophy - you don't get to keep it unless you win it three times in a row. You had to bring it back to give to the winner of this year's event.* According to Dick, Harry grinned, and replied, *Well, I'd better win it again because I've clean forgotten it.* The 36 holes were played in rain squalls and a high wind but Harry swept around the course with a 71 and a 70 to win the cup with a record score and an unprecedented winning margin of thirteen strokes.

Now that he was seventeen, the image of Harry that the press presented to the public changed. He was no longer a shy boy prodigy but an unpretentious young man of great talent. The story of his victory at Sorrento supported the impression of Harry as a young man, arguably the best golfer in Australia, who could decide to play dazzling golf and to do so at will. While everyone else recognised golf as periods of peaks and troughs which they had to learn to control by discipline, Harry possessed the skill to ignore this reality and to create his own peaks.

The cause for Harry's success, neglecting to bring the trophy, was another dimension to the story. It was not that Harry was oblivious to his position as an elite amateur golfer but that much of the pomp and circumstance surrounding the sport held little appeal. He did not immerse himself in the protocols of golf inherited from the Royal and Ancient. As Harry was not loquacious, his brief but cogent responses to questions from the press created the impression of him as imperturbable in his approach to the sport and affable in his outlook on life.

As 1933 unfolded Harry had a burst of blistering golf. In April, he broke the course record at Victoria winning the medal in a par competition with seven up playing off a plus two handicap. In July, he created a course record of 63 at Sorrento with twelve pars and six birdies. He won the Victoria Golf Club Championship and appeared set to take on all-comers.

It was a particularly wet and nasty winter in 1933 but a circle of men, snugly sitting in the warmth of the bar after their Saturday competition, watched the rain from the other side of the glass and discussed the forthcoming championships. Gus Jackson was adamant that golf in Australia was a whole new kettle of fish.

It's a fact. Each year in this country, golf championships are becoming more difficult to win. The standard of the game is higher than it was, is getting higher and there are more serious contenders for the big honors.

The bridal group at St Paul's Cathedral.
From left to right: Master Harry Williams age 8, Miss Beryl Admans, the bride
formerly Miss Thelma Williams, Miss Eileen Lake and Miss Annie Evans.
Table Talk, 20 September 1923.   Photo: Courtesy Eileen Grigg.

Harry age 12 in Brighton Grammar School uniform, 1927.
Photo: Courtesy Australian Golf Union Museum.

Young champion of the links - Harry Williams, 13 of Commonwealth Club who won the July medal on Saturday with 4 up.

Photo: Courtesy *The Sun News-Pictorial*, 24 July 1928.

COMMONWEALTH GOLF CLUB

HANDICAP STROKE | BOGE

Player: *H L Williams*   Date *13/9/29*   2

HOLES	Yards	BOGEY OR SCRATCH SCORE	Strokes Match or Bogey	PLAYER Strokes	+Won −Lost 0 Half	SELF Strokes	+Won −Lost 0 Half
1	344	4	9	4			
2	401	4	4	3			
3	126	3	16	2			
4	466	5	7	4			
5	500	5	1	6			
6	425	5	8	3			
7	403	5	11	3			
8	230	4	18	4			
9	484	5	3	5			
OUT	3379	40		34			
10	413	5	10	5			
11	320	4	14	4			
12	390	4	5	4			
13	517	5	2	6			
14	186	3	13	2			
15	462	5	6	5			
16	330	4	17	4			
17	150	3	15	2			
18	408	5	12	4			
IN	3176	38		36			
OUT	3379	40		34			
TOTAL	6555	78		70			

Total Against Bogey— Up Down

Deduct Handicap

Net Total - -

Signature of Marker: *E L Williams*

Top: Harry age 14, studio photograph, 1929. Photo: Courtesy Phil Tresidder's
Great Days of Australian Golf.
Bottom: Score card for Harry age 14 (handicap 2) showing a score of 70 strokes
around Commonwealth. Card signed by his father, 13 September 1929.

Harry age 21 at the top of his back-swing during the Australian Open at Metropolitan, 1936.

CELEBRITIES IN CAMEO
No. 1—Harry Williams

HARRY WILLIAMS, who ran Gene Sarazen, U.S.A. golf professional to four strokes in the Australian Open Golf Championship at Metropolitan on Saturday, is. at 21, still only a good three-years-old with his best golf in front of him.

He has been collecting titles since he first won the State amateur title in 1931 at Victoria links in rather sensational fashion. He was all of 16 then.

He is said to be the longest hitter of a golf ball that Victoria has had, and his height and apparently steely strong wrists are vital factors in helping him reach great lengths. More important still is his temperament. He is as evenly balanced as a veteran.

Top: Harry age 21 by cartoonist A. Stuart Peterson.
Photo: Courtesy *Table Talk*, 1 October 1936, State Library of Victoria.
Bottom: Harry age 21, being congratulated by runner-up Mick Ryan after winning the Victorian Amateur championship for the fourth time in 1936.
Photo: Courtesy *The Australasian*, 12 September 1936, State Library of Victoria.

Gene Sarazen during his second visit to Melbourne when he won the Australian Open at Metropolitan, 1936.

The picture is signed,
To Harry Williams
The Best Left Handed Golfer
in the <u>World</u>
Good Luck from Gene Sarazen.

Helen Hicks, first American woman professional golfer to play in Australia, who visited Melbourne with Gene and Mary Sarazen, 1936.

The picture is signed,
To - Harry Williams
With best wishes
Helen Hicks.

Photos: Courtesy Victoria Golf Club.

Harry age 21 with (l to r) his mother Doll, an unknown admirer and cousins Marie and Eileen at Kingston Heath, 1935 where Harry won the Victoria Amateur title. The photograph appeared in *The Sun News-Pictorial*.

Photo: Courtesy Eileen Grigg.

Caricatures of golfing personalities by Roy Dalgarno accompanying article by John Dillon on the Australian Open championship played at Metropolitan and won by Gene Sarazen. Harry age 21 was runner-up and leading amateur.

The two combatants: Harry with Jim Ferrier both age 18.
  Photo: Courtesy *The Australian Golf & Tennis Magazine*, 2 April 1934.

Front page of *The Sun News-Pictorial* featuring Harry age 16 the day after defeating ex-holder Mick Ryan for the Victorian Amateur championship.
Photo: Courtesy *The Sun News-Pictorial*, 8 August 1931,
State Library of Victoria.

Harry age 16 admiring the Victorian Amateur championship trophy after winning it the first time, 1931.

Photo: Courtesy Victoria Golf Club.

Harry age 16, at the top of his follow-through, 1931.
Photo: Courtesy Victoria Golf Club.

Victorian state team in Sydney, 1931.

L to r: Charlie Smith, Alec Russell, Harry age 16, Ivo Whitton, Henry Schlapp, Mick Ryan (capt.), L.M. McPherson.

Photo: Courtesy Victoria Golf Club.

GOOD COMPANIONS. Happy is the man who has friendship. Here in this free and independent land of ours he has been paid the finest tribute one man can pay another. It is a grand thing to share with good companions the good things of life. After a job well done, or a day of leisure enjoyed to the full, there is deep contentment in drinking with them a glass of **FOSTER'S LAGER**. In its golden glow is the very spirit of friendship. In its mellowness is the good companionship of Australia's finest barley, malt and hops ... brewed with the skilful care that has made **FOSTER'S** "Australia's National Beverage."

Advertisement for Foster's Lager depicting affluent, ruggedly handsome, Australian men playing golf "in this free and independent land of ours". Foster's Advertising - Sporting Series, September 1939.

Top: The dapper Norman Von Nida age 25 hitting off at Concord, Sydney, 1939.
Photo: Courtesy *The Von Nida Story*, Weldon Publishing.
Bottom: Harry age 24 on the 1st tee during the Phillipines Open in January 1940.
Photo: Courtesy Eileen Grigg.

Who would you put amongst your serious contenders? asked one of the circle, settling down for a pleasant session of banter and speculation. *Of course, there's Ivo and Mick and Harry and then on their day, you could name any number of others.*

Each year, though, new players are breaking through. I'm not saying that Ivo won't hold his own in the future but now, at every club there are young golfers who have the potential skill to come up and dispose of the established best performers. Look at this young Alex Rae. The young golfers of these days have advantages of well-maintained courses and help, both amateur and professional, that few of the older men in the game enjoyed.

But a lot of these youngsters won't stay around, announced one of the older men, *they're all fire and brimstone when they start out but, give them a few tough games and then we'll see only froth and bubble.*

Don't believe that, laughed Gus, *Once these new men get a taste of victory, and convince themselves of their quality, they'll bound ahead. Look at Harry. Look at the way he plays so confidently because he has won major events. Now he's taken out the Club championship here at Victoria.*

But will he keep going?

The men pondered this question seriously. In the pennant the next Saturday, Harry, playing number one for Victoria, was drawn against Mick Ryan, playing number one for Kingston Heath. Again, the match was being treated as a morality play of two styles of golf - the brilliant youth playing the seasoned campaigner. Gus ventured his opinion.

In my view, the real champions are those who don't wait for the inspiration of success. Some of the younger players I watch are crushed when they fail. They won't go on in the long term. With others, these setbacks spur them on to greater efforts. They seize on their failure to motivate them to strive to make amends. Only the fighter will get on in the game. That's what I like about Jim Ferrier. He's got a terrible swing but he keeps in there and works on it.

91

For a while the conversation was diverted into discussing Jim Ferrier but, as most of them had only seen him in the *Movietone* or *Cinesound* newsreels, they soon returned to the local scene where it was Mick Ryan who was widely regarded as a renowned fighter to the end. Gus again entered the fray.

In the championships, there is such an element of luck that no player should attach too much importance to their success. Success should be taken as a pleasant and perhaps lucky adventure.

A certain amount of disbelief greeted this statement.

You don't think the winners of the championships are the best golfers? I suppose I do mean that. Certainly, good golfers win the championship but it is the golfer who is the steady golfer over time who I think is the best. Only the fighter will get on in the game.

I can't agree with that, said one of the men with feeling. *I reckon I'm one of the most hard-fighting golfers in this club and I've never met with success yet.*

Everyone laughed. But another added,

That's exactly my point. The best golfer is the one who plays the best golf and, in my books, by far the best golf I've seen played on this course is today's round by Harry.

There was general assent.

Harry may not be so very much ahead of any other first-class players in the long game. But in that vital area around the green, where the average player needs three shots to get down, Harry is a master, and more than any other player in the land makes three shots into two. He's also the best putter among the cracks here now. Anyway, what he's already done in the game should be sufficient to answer anyone who thought that he wouldn't last.

The final words were accompanied with a questioning look around the audience as though he thought they had been of that opinion. Taking an appeasing role, the man on his left moved the discussion to Mick Ryan's golf.

If you go on form, Ryan should win. He is the current Australian Open champion, his game is very solid and the match will be played at Kingston Heath, where he is champion.

Harry's supporter interjected. *Harry's on his game too. If you'd seen him this afternoon, you'd back him. Brilliant golf will always beat steady golf. Just look at his score.*

The recounting of Harry's scores on the respective holes reminded the men of their own golf. They fell to comparing and contrasting their scores and then to a lengthy but exceedingly pleasing post-mortem of the vagaries of themselves, the disposition of the course, as if it were animate, and the whims of fortune.

On the Wednesday before the Victoria versus Kingston Heath pennant match, the *Sporting Globe* ran a major story, Stars Of Links In Big Attraction. Ryan and Williams To Meet. A large gallery turned out but, in the event, everyone was disappointed. On the Saturday 29 July, Mick Ryan had a severe bout of influenza. The 'flu that winter was severe for Eric Williams also contracted it later that month.

Instead of throwing the 'flu off, Eric began to complain of pains in the chest and that he was hot and shivery. The doctor was called and announced that Eric had developed pneumonia. The doctor reassured Doll that there was about 90% chance of him getting over it but, quietly, he also said, that they would just have to hope for the best as there was no really effective treatment for pneumonia.

Eric's condition worsened. When he coughed, there was blood on the towel with which he wiped his lips and he would cough until he lay exhausted. Eric recognised the worst, he was surely dying. He would have to put his affairs in order. Doll called their solicitor who arranged to come the next day. At this point, Eric still had rational periods and was able to talk over the future with Doll. When it came to looking after

Harry, they even admitted the possibility that Doll could be pregnant, allowing in the will for any other issue.

It appeared to Harry, that once his father signed his Will he gave up on life. Each day brought deterioration and then a plateau and then a further decline. But it was all towards death. On Friday 1 September 1933, just before midnight, Eric died, at the age of thirty-nine. At the house, as it became clear that the pneumonia threatened Eric's life, there had been a succession of people - his mother and sister, Thelma, Queenie with Harold and Eileen and Marie - to support and console. Harry found that the rituals of death were explicit and he agreed with those who came to pay their respects that, as a young man, it was now his duty to look after his mother.

But more pressing was the issue of playing in the national championships that began on the weekend. When Eric died on the Friday, Doll sought Jack Dillon's advice on the etiquette of the situation. Jack was reassuring. It would not show any disrespect for his father, he thought if Harry played after the funeral. Harry pulled out of the Mixed Foursomes on the Saturday and the Foursomes on the Monday. Doll was gratified to see that Jack included reference to Eric's death in his front-page article in the *Sporting Globe* that week and supported the view that Harry should still be part of the field.

After the funeral, Harry decided he would play in the Open that began on Thursday 7 September. Indeed, Doll encouraged Harry to occupy himself with his golf in the national titles for, as a leading amateur, he was an important figure in the championships. In the Open, Harry qualified amongst the top sixteen amateurs to play in the Amateur championship that followed. By the time the Amateur Championship began, Harry was settling into the tournament. However, Willie Hope, from Scotland, who had been the leading amateur in the 1932 British Open and had

94

recently arrived in Melbourne and joined Yarra Yarra, won the event from Gus Jackson very comfortably.

The 1933 Victorian Amateur championship played at Metropolitan in October completed the season. In the first round, Harry played brilliantly throughout the day, hitting the ball great distance and accurately. He was putting well, too, and followed a 74 in the morning with a 68 in the afternoon. There were many purple patches of wonderful play. According to one observer, Harry could do no wrong. In the high wind of the second round, he gave one of the greatest exhibitions yet seen in Australia of ball control and powerful hitting. Gus Jackson, however, defeated Harry in the final to win the title.

These years confirmed Harry's stature as a golfer. Over the period, he carved his name in the record books of numerous courses around Melbourne. He played golf that delighted those who followed him. The length of his drives and the accuracy of his long irons on to the green to stop within a yard of the pin astonished. But Harry also left his boyhood days behind him. When Gus Jackson won the Victorian Amateur title, he acknowledged Harry as the better golfer and added *This boy Williams is a man on and off the course*. As a lean, six-footer with a pleasing grin, Harry was also the picture of an Australian male. In referring to Harry's agreeable company, Jackson welcomed Harry into the camaraderie of the clubhouse. *There is not much fun in beating an opponent of his disposition and the members of the Victoria Golf Club, to a man, are proud of him.*

11

By 1933, Harry, as a foremost golfer in Australia, was in the middle of far-reaching changes to the sport and its culture. It was the considered opinion of many that Harry Williams was the best golfer in Australia at the time. But, at the time, the organisation of the sport defied any accurate assessment. The elite golfers might meet annually in the Australian Open championship but they existed in two different worlds. The divisions between the amateur and the professional golfer were as culturally rigid as they were financial.

During the early 1930s, the general improvement in the standard of golf was recognised by the demise of playing to bogey. It was said, in defence of the more demanding figure, that balls were travelling further, that the steel-shafted clubs hit further and more accurately and that golf courses had improved and were maintained more carefully. Bill Edgar, in an interview in December 1931 in *Golf* admitted that watching Harry play with steel-shafted clubs had been *a real eye-opener,* for he was getting the same distance with a 5-iron as Bill was with a 2-iron. More and more golfers carried a full range of graded irons, although a few eccentrics, George Fawcett, for instance, continued to play with only a 2-wood and a mid-iron.

From 1 January 1933, all golf clubs in Britain had agreed to play to par rather than bogey and by 1 January 1935, the same policy was in place in Melbourne. Several clubs had revised their standard scratch score already, now all clubs were brought into order. A number of leading amateurs visited the courses and set the standard scratch scores. It was determined that men drove 200 yards for a drive and 185 yards for a 2-wood second shot. The run differed between courses but on the sandbelt it was considered to be about twenty-five yards. In addition to these

96

estimates, allowance was given for degree of difficulty of the general layout of the course, its bunkers and other hazards.

Don Thompson, golf instructor at London Stores commented that, as professionals had to play off scratch, they would continue to do so. For Harry, too, playing off plus two, the new standards were of little concern. At the elite level, other pressures existed. In Australia, the division between professionals and amateurs was an intrinsic part of the game. Each had its own rationale. In the culture of the sport, however, amateur golf was accorded higher status than professional golf. Yet, the amateur golfers were generally not the best golfers. The barriers between the two appeared insurmountable.

In September 1933, these tensions generated much of the interest in the outcome of the Australian Open. On the surface it was a competition between individual golfers but underlying the day to day events was a keen contest between the professionals and the amateurs. For the first time in the playing of golf in Australia, the leading amateur players were in the same class as, and could at least hold their own with the best professionals. Although the professionals had taken eight of the thirteen titles contested since the war, amateurs had won three of the last four championships. The foremost professionals approached the championship at Royal Melbourne, serious in their intent to regain the title but, as it stood, Mick Ryan was favourite and Ivo Whitton was next to him in the betting. Harry Williams, because of his recent bereavement was considered out of the running. The rivalry between the two camps, always beneath the surface at the Open, became more overt.

The Championship opened in wet and windy conditions. Harry played as well as could be expected but was not amongst the leaders. Mick Ryan hit off at 9 a.m. in the worst of the weather on the first round and his 84 virtually ended his chances. Ivo Whitton played convincing golf in

97

the stormy winds of Thursday for a 78, and followed that up with a worthy 75 on Friday, when he stood first favourite for the title. But the loss of his ball on the very first shot on Saturday morning, threw him off his play, and his 45 out was fatal. However, Jim Ferrier and Gus Jackson were still in the running after the first three rounds.

On the Tuesday before the 1933 Open championship began, the professionals' interstate game had taken place and Lou Kelly, the twenty-year old professional from Goulburn had gone round in 69. Bill Corry and Tommy Heard, two of the New South Wales professionals, observed this with interest. They recognised that here was a golfer in good form, the most likely contender for the Open from the professionals, one worthwhile putting some money on. There was, however, the uncertainty of a novice like Kelly remaining relaxed as the pressures of the competition mounted. They decided to take him in hand. Bill would be his mentor. He took Kelly aside and advised him.

Just concentrate on each hole as a hole and play for the par figure at each hole. You've got the golf to win. You can do it. Certainly, you'll miss par on some holes but against that there will be holes where luck'll come in and you'll get birdies. And if you miss perfect figures on those holes, others will be missing them too.

After a couple of holes in the opening round, Kelly remembered the advice and settled down to go after pars and to think only of the hole he was playing. His 73 in the difficult conditions of the day put him at the front of the field.

That evening, Bill Corry returned with more advice for the second round.

You're in front. Keep on the way you're going; forget everything else; let them do the worrying. They'll have to chase you.

Kelly scored 76 while the rest of field did chase him and, at the end of the day, his lead had diminished. Bill and Tommy redoubled their efforts. They took Kelly for a long walk and kept him amused with stories of their lives so he would be really tired and ready for bed and to sleep.

They were successful and Kelly went out for the third round ready to keep his mind on par and on each hole as a separate entity. He third and fourth rounds of 73 and 80 gave him the Open. Jim Ferrier was second for the second successive time.

Lou Kelly was extremely grateful to Bill for guiding him through the rigours of the event. He realised his good fortune. Winning the Open would set him up for life. Since he was fourteen, he had worked as assistant to the professional, Jack Irving, at Royal Canberra. He had done all the jobs - mended clubs, looked after members, tended the greens - and in any time he had left over, he had practised. Irving had sent him to Sydney to compete in the assistant professionals' tournament, which he had won. On the strength of this, he had obtained the position of professional at Goulburn.

There were showers during the last round and someone borrowed Harry's mackintosh for Lou Kelly to put round his shoulders. When Kelly returned it, Harry wished him well. Neither of them recognised each other as equals. Lou Kelly knew himself as an employee. Harry Williams played golf as a member of a club. Kelly considered golf an occupation, for Harry golf was meant to be a complement to a career. Kelly subscribed to a professional association whereas Harry's golfing partners comprised a more amorphous network, sharing a common outlook maybe but from a range of business and professional fields of expertise. Kelly, as an apprentice, depended on a mentor such as Jack Irving at Royal Canberra. Eric, in overseeing Harry's entry into golf and Doll, who never missed following a game, were outside the sport and lacked influence and hence credibility. They were two very different perspectives on playing the game of golf.

When Kelly accepted the trophy, he adopted a suitably modest stance in receiving the award. His period of apprenticeship had taught him to be unassuming publicly about his golfing achievements. He claimed that he was lucky to win - *Someone had to be the winner - I was lucky - and I am not ashamed to say that I am very glad about it* - and proceeded to thank everyone who had contributed to his success. Kelly was hailed as one of the cleanest living golfers around. He had not tasted - did not intend to taste - strong drink, was essentially modest and deeply religious, and viewed his success more as a pleasing thing for his widowed mother than as a meritorious thing that he had done.

However, an indication of changes in the perception of golf surfaced with the Victorian Centenary golfing event held in 1934. Until then, with some diversions, the amateur world of golf, holding to the authority of the Royal and Ancient St Andrews, held sway. But, in 1934, golf, as it was played in the United States, challenged this model. Although amateur golf was important in the United States, golf there was usually equated with professional golfers as very marketable individuals. They were recognised as the best, they were paid accordingly and they generated most publicity about the sport. In an interview with *Golf* in 1935, Gene Sarazen put the case succinctly, *Let's be honest. We play golf for money. We are in it for a profession. We work at it as a man does a job.* In 1934, this view of golf was given tangible expression in the Victorian Centenary Golf tournament and Melburnians loved it.

In 1934, Victoria celebrated one hundred years of European settlement dating from the day Batman sailed up the Yarra and stated his intention of establishing a village. Late in 1932, the Victorian Golf Association was approached by the Centenary Committee to consider how they might contribute to the celebrations. They immediately thought of a visit from a British amateur team to play in Victoria. By July 1933 this proposal had broadened. There would be a tournament with £5,000 prize money to attract big name players from the United States. Sidney Myer, as a prominent businessman, was on the Centenary committee. He had taken up golf in the United States in the 1920s and although, as a Jew, he was unacceptable in certain golf clubs around Melbourne - he was a member at Commonwealth, Yarra Yarra and Kew - promised £500 towards the prize money. The British team of amateur golfers assumed minor importance, they would also be invited and they would play inter-Empire matches while they were here.

Planning for the Centenary events showed the place of different sports within the Melbourne sporting culture and that golf occupied an ambivalent role. In the program, there was a division between sports that offered prize money and those that were strictly amateur. For racing, the total stakes to be provided over the season was nearly £100,000, for the cycling event prize money amounted to £2,400 together with a gold cup valued at £105 given by Sidney Myer and for the light car event, £5,000. For baseball, a White Sox team was invited from the United States and promised 75% of the gate money. Tennis, by contrast, remained outside the marketplace and the two best male players at the time, Fred Perry of Britain and Jack Crawford of New South Wales, were both to attend without financial incentive.

At the beginning of 1934, the VGA, under the presidency of H. G. McRoberts, and the Metropolitan Golf Club, where the event was to be held, reported that prize money of £3,000 was assured - donations of £500 from Metropolitan and £300 from the Nicholas family had secured the event. The prize money - £1,000 first prize and another £1,000 distributed to the first fifteen professionals - was designed, primarily, to attract professional golfers. As the organisers stated, *This is one of the largest purses ever offered in the history of Australian golf and is expected to attract some of the world's greatest golfers.* The professional tournament the following week, when another £500 first prize and £500 to the rest was to be distributed added further incentive to the professional golfer to play.

101

Such a venture was revolutionary to those whose ideas of golf were still of stout aging males huffing and puffing their way around a golf course with two or three clubs. A. S. Howcroft writing in the Saturday *Argus* of 18 August 1934 on the Popularity of Golf still found it difficult to accept that golf was no longer *an old man's game*. He lamented, *if one is aged more than 18 or 20 years one is in danger of being pushed to the wall in the helter-skelter after 'birdies' and 'eagles'*. He did, however, take comfort in the continued success of the Honourable Michael Scott, by then in his mid- fifties. At the same time, Jack Dillon in the *Sporting Globe* entered the debate with an article headed, Money Enters Golf. Is This Change For Good Or For Evil? The venture also offended the purists. So absolute was the British sense of amateur golf, a view echoed by parts of the Melbourne golfing fraternity, that the editor of *Golf Illustrated* criticised the organisers for presenting a gold cup to the winning amateur, arguing that this infringed their amateur status. Such awards would only contaminate amateur golf.

Invitations were extended to the United States and to St Andrews. By March, a group of six players from the US was definite. Reservations about the American professional and the sensitivity of Victorian golfing circles sustained the committee in submitting a list of players who would be welcome. The British team was announced, J. W. Trumble, member of Royal Melbourne and St Andrews and former Test cricketer having been instrumental in the arrangements. The visiting British amateur team was to be led by The Honourable Michael Scott and, according to Trumble, they were *a fine lot of fellows (who) should be very popular in Australia*. They were to be accommodated at Victoria Golf Club during their stay. In September, when the US players were announced, there were reassurances that they were also *high-class citizens*. The manager of the USPGA, Mr Robert Harlow, reassured the press that the men were fine ambassadors of the game. *I wish to assure the Australian golf world that the six men we are sending are not only the champions of American golf, but are personally high-class citizens whose actions on the golf course, in the locker-room, and elsewhere speak for themselves.*

Indeed, the US professionals could have been amateurs. Harlow continued, *The worthwhile angle of the whole venture is its contribution to international sport. I wish to emphasise as strongly as possible that this is not a commercial undertaking. These men are giving three months of their time and guarantees to comply with a request that can mean no more to them than expenses.* At the same time, Gene Sarazen and Joe Kirkwood, who were also invited to the tournament, arrived and began a series of exhibition matches. The commercial aspect of their visit could not be denied. In October they were barred from playing any matches in the metropolitan area until after the Centenary meeting. As the President of the VGA explained, more than £4,500 had been required to bring the visitors to Australia and they did not want them to their reduce their novelty value. It was also a little misleading to consider the US professionals as not benefiting financially from the visit for they decided to split prize and other monies between them equally.

Australians already knew Joe Kirkwood but the appearance of Gene Sarazen was greeted with much interest. Famous for his plus fours and for his style generally, Gene Sarazen was at the peak of his golfing career. In 1932, he had led from start to finish of the British Open to win it comfortably. He won a third USPGA title in 1933 and in 1934 was runner-up in the US Open. In Australia, as he went round the country playing exhibition matches, there was much to admire. He regularly played well. He recovered from trouble without fail. He was the consummate golfer and attracted large crowds to exhibition games, which he and Kirkwood played as they made their way to the Centenary tournament. They reached Melbourne early in November and appeared at the Myer Mural Dining Hall, where, for 1/- the public was invited *to see these two world-famous American celebrities of the Golf World.*

The American professionals took the Australian golfing world by storm. Craig Wood, Paul Runyan, Densmere Shute, Harry Cooper, Leo Diegel, Ky Laffoon as well as Gene Sarazen and the expatriate Joe Kirkwood. Jack Dillon in the *Sporting Globe* entitled the American visitors, *the invaders*, apparently accepting the British team as part of the Australian golfing circle. At the Australian Open championship in Sydney in August, Bill Bolger won the title from Gene Sarazen before a gallery of 3,000. The publicity mounted. The Centenary Event, it was claimed in the press, was the greatest ever arranged outside Great Britain and America and testified to the acceptance of golf as an appropriate sport, *not only for the leisured few, but also for the masses.*

The American visitors proved huge draw cards. The Centenary tournament attracted a crowd of over 4,000. The Americans became identities: Paul Runyan, billed as the farmer's boy from Arkansas; Ky Laffoon's claim was his Cherokee descent; Densmere Shute, the American-born son of English parents; Craig Wood, a big, blonde, handsome American college man; Joe Ezar, dressed in a black beret, blue trousers and yellow tie, who wisecracked his way around the course, was supposedly Syrian but came from Texas. Then of course, there was Gene Sarazen, a pocket Hercules swapping jokes with the gallery.

The Americans' bright and colourful clothes and their slacks rather than plus fours surprised and delighted. Members of the tour were much photographed as evidence of American style. Their conversation was reported verbatim, the American drawl further evidence of the exotic. Their wives were interviewed as instant experts on world fashion and films. When Jimmy Thomson won, he turned two somersaults on the green. By then, this behaviour was accepted as exuberance and the US professionals were pronounced a great success.

Their departure left a less settled Australian golf scene. Most media attention had centred on the American entourage. At the Centenary Open, the American professional had captured the headlines. No longer was it assumed that the British style of organising golf was the only way. Within the golfing circles Harry moved, however, the British model continued to occupy centre stage and talks of developing a more regular competition between Australian and British amateur teams became more serious.

But in the public forums of the nation, the allure of golf as it was played in the United States had been heeded. The 1934 Centenary showed that golf, as a spectator sport, had arrived. By now, golf had been integrated into the spectating culture of the city. Melburnians had shown they were both prepared to watch golf generally, rather than just a specific name player, and to return on successive occasions. In Melbourne, for the final round of the State Amateur title in October 1932, the decision to charge members of the gallery 2/- placed amateur golf firmly in the marketplace. Prizes and prize monies could be increased and the best players who might profit from the development could not be neatly separated into a rigid division of the amateur gentleman and the professional employee.

During the series of golfing events encompassed by the Victorian centenary, Harry had played well. In the match between Britain and Australia at Royal Melbourne, he had been brilliant. Indeed, Jack McLean, a member of the British amateur team and winner of the Amateur event at the Centenary tournament, wrote to Harry from on board the H.M.S. Niagara on his way back to Scotland, *I hope a team will be sent home in the near future, if it is, you will be in that team.* Although this recommendation gave immense personal satisfaction to Harry, it was completely overshadowed in the public golfing arena by the sensation of the American professionals.

12

While the politics of the golfing world bubbled along, Harry was constructing his own version of adult life. Up until now, Harry as a teenager had been dependent on his parents for financial support and this had been given without question. Just as Harry was making the transition from schooldays to the workforce, Eric died. With his father's death, the conditions under which Harry played golf changed considerably.

When Eric's will was read, Doll and Harry were left a comfortable estate. There was the newsagency - the shop and the goodwill - and there was Eric's share in his father's estate. It amounted to £13,200. In 1934, it was estimated that a two-bedroom brick house cost approximately £1,000 to build. The will left the income of half the estate to Doll for her lifetime and the other half of the estate to Harry on his attaining the age of twenty-one and the rest of the estate coming to him on the death of his mother.

After Eric's death, Doll had been ill and Harry had taken more responsibility in the business. In the Victorian Amateur title in October 1933, Harry was reported to be working four hours before appearing at Metropolitan for his hit-off time in the championships. For an eighteen-year-old, with little experience, this was a difficult period. Harry and Doll decided that the newsagency was definitely not the career he wanted. But he needed some occupation. Through his network of golfing associates, Harry landed a position in insurance. This work combined with his golf most agreeably.

Moving into insurance was relatively easy. Playing golf, Harry was often in a good position to talk with other golfers about their affairs and to sell insurance to them if they were interested. At the time, Don Thompson, the golf instructor at London Stores, when addressing the *Argus* luncheon told his audience, *The man who plays the game on the links will play it in business too*. As Harry knew, he could never be accused of being either a sneak or bad tempered in golf, the characteristics disliked in business as on the golf course. So he proffered his services to the insurance industry with confidence. Due to the good services of Dick Payne, he was given the insurance for Victoria Golf Club. Harry could claim that he was an insurance inspector.

Harry, as a celebrity and an agreeable young man, was socially acceptable. He now had a car and was not tied down to any nine to five job. At the time, Sir John Latham, then attorney-general but appointed chief justice of the High Court in 1935, was reported as asking rhetorically, Is Melbourne Dull? He found that the answer was unequivocally in the affirmative. Indeed, it was the funerals of Nellie Melba and John Monash in 1931 and Sidney Myer in 1934 that perhaps best expressed Melbourne's public life in the period. Large crowds waited quietly and respectfully for the corteges to pass and then dispersed to their suburban homes for an early night.

To a visitor, Melbourne offered few diversions at night and almost none on Sundays. Dancing and music were curtailed by legal restrictions related to the serving of food and liquor. Hotels closed at 6 p.m. and in dining rooms of even the best hotels - the Oriental, Scott's, the Occidental, the Australia, the Old Treasury, and Menzies - glasses had to be off the tables by 8 p.m. Sport, theatre and films were limited by restrictions on their hours of operation and, at the time, Sunday sport on public sites came under renewed attack.

For a fairly wealthy young man, however, the scene was not so limited. Melbourne's social life was based in the more private networks of large houses dotted around the affluent suburbs of the city and the holiday spots along the Bay. These were major sites for entertainment: tennis parties, dances to the piano, gramophone or small band, dinners and celebrating the different rites of passage of a family. Sometimes, these became significant social events. In December 1933, one and a half thousand guests arrived at St Paul's Cathedral for the marriage of Cynthia Brookes to the Lord Mayor of Melbourne, Sir Harold Gengoult Smith. After the ceremony they proceeded up Swanston Street to the reception at Town Hall and then to the ball at the Brookes's mansion 'Kurneh' in Domain Road. Late in the night, Dame Mabel Brookes and her helpers cut up a tier of the wedding cake and distributed it to the large crowd, waiting outside for a glimpse of the festivities.

On these social networks there was built a busy public calendar of activity: the races, tennis at Kooyong, rowing regattas, the golf championships. Then, there were acceptable nightspots, Mario's, the Ritz, Ricco's, Navoretti's. The Chevron Hotel, recently opened in St Kilda Road, was a welcome sign of some lightening of the gloom of depression. Generally, the controls in place could be circumvented and, knowing the right person to ask for when knocking on the door of a hotel after 6 p.m. or the right drinks to order was advantageous to the continuation of the high spirits of the party.

Harry, by birth and social position, was not automatically part of this charmed set who provided the material for the weekly issues of *Table Talk*. However, as Amateur Golf Champion, his sporting prowess was a social key. He was tall, good looking and pleasant. The series of tournaments over summer such as the Sorrento Cup were part of Melbourne's summer social calendar. Hostesses vied with each other to accommodate the golfers and to entertain them well. Harry, too, was a good tennis player and always welcome to join any tennis party that was organised. Nevertheless, Harry did not become a social lion. He was not a great conversationalist who could readily flatter the mothers and charm the daughters. Nor was he an enthusiastic dancer so he did not seek out the social occasions where he may be required to perform eloquently or to foxtrot his way gracefully around the floor.

What most appealed to Harry were the races. Eric and Doll had gone to the races and when Eric died Doll expected Harry to escort her to the major events of the racing calendar. Harry liked the horses and, when there were major golf events during the week, he was able to go to the races on Saturdays and on Wednesdays when mid-week racing was held. By now, after the closure of Sandown, Fitzroy and Aspendale racetracks in 1931 and Richmond in 1932, horse-racing was more concentrated. Caulfield was particularly convenient but he found that Moonee Valley and Flemington each had their charms, Moonee Valley was more intimate and the members' enclosure at Flemington was a pleasant area. Harry and Doll rarely went further than the big three though the Williamstown Cup was sometimes considered.

Harry also enjoyed the dinners and parties that were based on his circle of golfing acquaintances. There were Sportsmen's Nights where a table at the Society in Bourke Street was organised with a menu - hors d'oeuvres, vegetable soup, spaghetti neapolitan, fillets of whiting, cutlets milanese, quail, pancakes and coffee - offering substantial fare for Australian palates. Alternatively, a group of friends would book a table for a buck's night at the Latin in Lonsdale Street, being particularly daring by opening proceedings with Mae West cocktails. For a lavish occasion, there was Florentino's in Bourke Street. At these gatherings, Harry was not a great storyteller but he appreciated a good story and contributed the wry comment to the conversation.

Alcohol was a normal part of the social scene. Seppelts Fine Wines and McWilliams Sherries appeared on menus in the city restaurants but generally, beer and spirits were the main drinks in the clubhouse. By now, the first experiments with alcohol as a schoolboy had been consolidated and Harry found he could drink quite comfortably with the older men with whom he played golf. It was part of the agreeable rituals of the game, and especially for a new boy joining the circle, promoted a feeling of confident well being.

In 1934, Harry turned nineteen and settled into the season, playing some ordinary rounds but others studded with bursts of wonderful golf. In January, although he played well, he just lost out to Willie Hope in the Sorrento Cup. In April, he retained his Club championship title at Victoria and won the Riversdale scratch golf event played on the Monday of the King's Birthday weekend.

When pennant began, Harry was captain of the team and he dropped himself to number two as a result of poor form. Then, he was knocked over by a bicycle crossing Barkly street and received bruises and cuts to his face and concussion. By the end of July, he had recovered. In August, when he finished equal third in the Geelong Centenary Golf championship, part of the Victorian Centenary celebrations, it had been, it was said, an *adventurous outing* but *with characteristic brilliance he reeled off some great holes*.

In August, the 1934 Australian Championships were held at Royal Sydney. W.J. (Billy) Bolger won the Open and in the Amateur Championship, Tom McKay was successful. At the tournament, Harry identified with the visiting British amateur team and was happy with both their company and the style of golf they represented. He played with Jack McLean, a genial Scot from Hayston Golf Club, Kirkintilloch, Glasgow. Jack McLean spoke authoritatively on golf and the *Sporting Globe* carried a front-page article by him on the state of the sport. Harry listened to him attentively and was impressed by Jack's belief that Harry would be welcome to play golf in Britain.

Back in Melbourne, in early September 1934, Harry swept all before him in the Victorian Amateur Championship and won the title by the widest margin in the history of the event. On Monday 4 September, the championship opened at Woodlands. Harry moved smoothly through the first two rounds and the semi-final, hardly drawing breath. In the final on the Thursday, Harry met Mick Ryan. In the morning, Harry scored 73, putting him five holes ahead. In the afternoon, he positively sparkled. He took 33 on the first nine holes, increasing his lead to nine holes, to be dormie. Then Ryan, with two pars, won the next two holes, keeping the score at dormie. On the 30th hole, Ryan drove long but Harry outdistanced him by twenty-five yards and played the 330 yards hole in three to win with six holes to spare. Harry had toyed with the field.

By September, no one in Melbourne could avoid the preparations for the centenary. Every organisation in the State was called on to contribute in some way or another and prominent businessmen such as Sidney Myer and Macpherson Robertson, by significant donations, ensured the events had international consequence. Certainly 1934 had its own quota of dramatic incidents. The news of the fifth test in August when Ponsford and Bradman scored a record 451 and Australia regained the Ashes occasioned much rejoicing and the notorious pyjama girl murder case provided a macabre riddle for those who followed its twists and turns. As the year advanced, Harry found that the events organised for the Centenary of the State of Victoria assumed sufficient momentum to push other news stories off the front page.

The celebration of Victoria's centenary broke the mould of the city's daily routines. Following the collapse of the boom of the late nineteenth century, the divisiveness of World War I and Depression, Melbourne public life had retreated beneath an overlay of inactivity and stifling conservatism. The celebration of the centenary forced the civic leaders

111

to adopt an active role. In July, when Sidney Myer, died, his funeral attracted immense crowds in recognition of his more enterprising style of public beneficence, part of which was the prize money for the Centenary golf tournament to be held in October.

Harry was as good as his word and took his mother to all the events she thought would be entertaining. After all, both the Halfeys and the Williams families had been pioneers, making them obvious participants in the commemoration of Batman's landing. For months there was debate about which of the royal Princes would be sent for the event and, in the end, it was Henry, Duke of Gloucester, who was given the task. Hardly effervescent, he nevertheless looked the part of an august member of the British Royal family as he swept past the crowd in Beaconsfield Parade on his way from Port Melbourne into the city.

They were also amongst the huge crowd that watched the arrival of Scott and Campbell Black to win the Centenary Air Race. In the crowd, talk of speeds of 200 miles an hour circulated and Harry marvelled at the fragility of the planes as they flew over Flemington to land at Laverton and the immensity of the distance they had travelled. Harry went to the start of the big cycle race that began outside Government House in the Domain and finished at Como Park a week later. He also went to see Walter Lindrum defend his world title at Lindrum's Billiard Parlour in Flinders Street. Then, there was an excursion with Doll to the Fitzroy Gardens to see what was purported to be Captain Cook's cottage, presented to the Victorian government by Russell Grimwade and now sitting, rather incongruously, amidst the flowerbeds and lawns.

Just as enjoyable as the big events, was the novelty of promenading in the city. Harry and Doll, several times, went in to walk the Golden Mile, lit up for the occasion by a brilliant display of the power of electricity. In her silk stockings, gloves and hat, tipped jauntily to one side and swathed in an eye veil, and carmine lipstick, Doll considered herself most chic and very much part of sophisticated life. Venetian poles or lolly sticks as they were quickly dubbed were spaced along the footpaths and lit up Bourke and Collins streets. More spectacular, the floodlighting of the major city buildings and monuments - the Town Hall, Flinders Street station, the Windsor Hotel, Parliament House, the Art Gallery - transformed the city into a glamorous theatre set. People flowed over Princes Bridge to Joyland; a fairground set up along Batman Avenue where they could view the Centenary Birthday Cake, all ten tons of it. What surprised Harry and Doll nearly as much as the flags, the decorations and the lights was the numbers of foreign people in the streets for ships of friendly nations had been invited to dock at Melbourne for the Centenary celebrations and sailors from every country mingled in the crowd.

In October, on a perfect day at the MCG, Richmond outplayed current premiers South Melbourne to become easy winners of the Centenary Grand Final. Despite four quick goals late in the game from Laurie Nash, who earlier in the year kicked eighteen for Victoria against South Australia, South could not curb the brilliance of Richmond's Jack (Skinny) Titus and the vigour of Jack (Captain Blood) Dyer. Doll was a keen Collingwood supporter while Harry favoured Melbourne but both agreed that Richmond's appearance in the last four grand finals was getting past a joke. At the end of the month, Harry himself became one of the major exhibits of the celebrations when he took part in the Centenary Golf Tournament. However, he was quite eclipsed by the notoriety of the visiting US professionals who captured all the headlines.

Harry was again back in the crowd when on 11 November, he and Doll were amongst the 300,000 who gathered around the Shrine of Remembrance. Harry had watched the building of the Shrine of Remembrance with interest. He liked the drive along St Kilda Road and he always took that way if he was going into the city for its broad expanse, its shady trees in summer and the mansions that lined it filled him with a sense of serenity. The new structure dominated the northerly aspect on his way into the city and the southerly aspect on the way out. At first, he resisted any change to the skyline but as it took shape, Harry accepted the Shrine as a new landmark for his city. The monument also appealed to him that it commemorated Anzac, an event that had taken place the same year as he was born. He was an Anzac baby.

And to make the whole year really memorable, there was an incredibly wet spring and early summer. In South Yarra, the recently formed Como Park was re-named Lake Como and water flooded the Kooyong tennis courts to the consternation of the organisers of the Centenary Tennis Tournament. Peter Pan won the Melbourne Cup on a sodden track - the picture hats and long light organdie and crepe dresses bedraggled by the heavy downpours of the afternoon. And at Victoria Golf Club, in December, after five days of rain, a large lake appeared between the 11th tee and the fairway. Many Victoria Club members, like Harry remembered the year as significant in marking the passing of time.

If the nineteen-year-old Harry saw 1934 as a year of change, it did not go unmarked by his colleagues. The enthusiasm of the Boy Wonder had been succeeded by the mastery of a top golfer. The dominant presence of Eric was no longer there. Although Eric had hindered rather than helped Harry's entry into the top golfing circles in Melbourne, he had been a strong influence in directing Harry's talents and in organising the family's affairs. Now, Doll was the lone voice. She was emotionally very demanding of Harry. Used to being the centre of attention, Harry could not bring friends to Mulgoa Street, Brighton without Doll taking over. While she enjoyed his success, Doll had no ambition for Harry to pursue further goals if it required changing her own pleasant routines.

Harry attempted to carve out his own life. Harry was out more and often it was early hours of the morning when he let himself in and crept quietly down the passage to his bedroom. Doll was worried that Harry was drinking. She pestered Harry, where was he going, was he drinking, why didn't he come home. He avoided confrontation. She confided to Queenie. Queenie reassured her that Harry was a young man and that he should be able to look after himself.

More than one well-meaning partner agreed that Harry had lost his zest for the game though whether this was the result of too much golf or a symptom of wider changes in Harry's life, they were not sure. In November, Jack Dillon, weighed in to the argument in the public columns of the *Sporting Globe* writing, *This brilliant left-hander needs a year's rest from serious golf, and my advice to him (and to his mother), is that he should take it.* Harry evidently took the advice for he did not feature in major competitive golf until the end of April when he defended his Club championship at Victoria.

13

By 1935, when Harry turned twenty, Harry had been playing top golf for seven years and was accepted as *a man on and off the course*. As a golfer, Harry was concerned with maintaining his place as one of Australia's best players and furthering his career. All golfers had periods when they did not play well or when others played better. Harry experienced these occasions. But there were signs that, at times, Harry had difficulty with controlling the sociability of his life as a top amateur golfer and a single young male. There was no denying his continued brilliance but reports of Harry's golf introduced words such as *erratic* to describe his play.

Golf was not a particularly physically exacting game and could accommodate a margin of indulgence. Therefore, excess was not necessarily evident nor was the outcome dramatic, just the setting in place of habits that would become very difficult to break and which, for some people, could set up a pattern of dependence. Similarly, following the horses, while acceptable as an interest, was not seen as a suitable career choice for an elite amateur golfer. But playing top golf continued to set the perimeters of Harry's life. Indeed, another round in the rivalry with Jim Ferrier once again emblazoned Harry's name in the annals of Australian golfing history.

Harry returned to competitive golf in 1935 *without much zest*, according to reports. He defended the Club championships at Victoria: in the first round he totalled 80, a figure normally out of bounds to him. Then in the next round, his 35 out for the first nine redeemed his chances. But he collapsed with a *hopeless* 41 home and Dick Payne won in what was termed a *more or less runaway victory*. Playing in the Riversdale

116

Scratch Event the next month Harry came in second and after that settled more into the golfing round. It was reported that although he had been *off his game for some time, he is returning to form*. When the national titles, played that year at Royal Adelaide in August, came round, however, Harry was reported not to be in good health and did not go.

In September, when the Victorian Amateur titles were held at Kingston Heath, Harry was a reluctant starter and Doll entered him in the event. At the time Mick Ryan won the Australian Open in 1932, he had taken the opportunity to put the case for Kingston Heath to be included in the list of championship courses. In 1934, the Club spent over £2,000 on improvements and in 1935 was rewarded with the Victorian Amateur Championship. According to Jack Dillon in the *Sporting* Globe, it was now *perhaps the greatest links in Australia*.

During the 1935 Victorian Amateur championship, Harry played some wonderful golf and he always had particularly fond recollections of the event. After the qualifying rounds, the match play began on Monday 9 September in brilliant weather. Harry's first opponent was Mick Ryan. Harry was out in 34, flawless apart from three putts on the 4th, and finished the morning two up. Lunch in the clubhouse offered the opportunity for a meal and a drink, the opportunity to break the stresses of match play. After the break, Harry lost the first three holes but then recovered to win one up. In the second round, Harry scored a magnificent 70 in the morning and was eight up on Geoff Grimwade at lunch. He finished him off at the 24th hole and had an early day.

The semi-final on the Wednesday was a gruelling contest. Harry played the redoubtable Willie Hope. In the morning, Hope rarely missed a chance of setting a stymie and Harry had spent much time considering these putts but had dealt with them effectively. The real tug of war began at the 34th hole in the afternoon. On the 34th, Harry's putt did not fall and Willie Hope sank his three-footer narrowing Harry's lead to one up with two to play. They halved the next hole. Hope was dormie one. On the 36th, Willie Hope had a fair drive but Harry hit a screamer, 50 yards farther. Hope's ball lay on an upward slope and, not allowing for this, his ball landed far to the left of the green. Meantime, Harry easily got the green and won the critical hole with a fine four. It was good to have a drink and relax at the end of it.

The final became a contest between two left-handers, Harry and Alex King, who was on his home course. Alex King appeared nervous to begin with and lost the first three holes so that he was six down at the end of the morning. It looked a foregone conclusion. But after lunch, Harry lost the first four holes and Alex King began to creep back into the game. By the 34th with three holes to go Harry was only one up. The 34th was a vital hole. Alex King pulled his drive to the rough, and his second, hitting a tree, lodged in a greenside bunker and Harry, winning, became dormie two.

The 35th settled it and became one of Harry's happiest memories. He always considered his second shot on the hole as one of the best of his career. The 459-yard 35th extended over a hill to a blind hole. Both players had good drives. On their second hit, Alex King played first and sent his full 2-wood to nine feet of the pin. The gallery, on the hill who could see the hole, cheered, certain that the game would go to the 36th. Then Harry played, using a 4-wood. Over the hill, the ball went, straight as an arrow, it landed, trickled down the hill and came to rest a yard inside the other ball. Gasps of amazement, then hearty applause. King putted first and down rolled his four-yarder. Then Harry putted and his ball also found the hole for three. They had halved the hole with eagle threes. Harry won the title, two up and one to play. Harry followed up this victory with a win in the 1935 Victorian Amateur Foursome championship with Dick Payne as his partner.

Meanwhile, Jim Ferrier, the other Boy Wonder of 1931, had let nothing divert him from devoting himself to golf. By the mid-1930s he was playing consistently well and had established himself as *Big Jim*, an authoritative figure on the golfing circuit. In the 1935 Australian Open at Royal Adelaide in August, Jim Ferrier finished behind Fergus McMahon after leading all the way. The crowd rallied to his gallant response to failure and *the thunder of applause that followed him was even greater than that given to the winner*. In commenting on his defeat, Jim Ferrier stated he was more sorry on behalf of his father who would be especially disappointed by his loss. However, he restored his father's happiness by winning the Australian Amateur title the next week at Royal Adelaide by defeating Harry Hattersley.

In October, Jim Ferrier was again in the headlines: Ferrier Breaks More Records. Aggregate Of 266 Thought To Be World's Best. In the Manly Close Tournament, Jim Ferrier had won by a margin of sixteen with a superb aggregate. His feat was reported across the nation. Here was Australia's best. In December, Ferrier announced his intention to further his career by going to play in the British championships and in February 1936 he left for England. Jim Ferrier's exploits overseas were constantly reported in the Australian press. He reached the final of the British Amateur Championship but lost to the Scot, Hector Thomson. He won the Silver Tassie at Gleneagles. Next he won *Golf Illustrated*'s Gold Vase. An Australian golfer had made it on the world stage.

When Jim Ferrier returned to Australia in August, he came back a golfing hero. It was said, *his adventure was the greatest and best. Out of that fire he undoubtedly came tried, tempered and bettered steel.* On the strength of his profile, Ferrier began writing columns for the *Sydney Morning Herald*, offering his personal viewpoint as a matter of significance. In any discussion of the relative merits of Jim Ferrier and Harry Williams five years on from the first meeting, the money was now decidedly with Jim Ferrier. The golfing afficionados expected the rivalry to be renewed in the forthcoming championships. Some suggested that Harry exercised a *hoodoo* over Ferrier. But those who knew Ferrier as Big Jim were quite sure there was no chink in his confidence or his subconscious where Harry or anyone else was concerned.

Meanwhile, at home, Harry had applied himself to golf when the 1936 season opened. If 1935 had been relatively desultory in terms of golf, Harry now played regularly and practised had. He began the new year in brilliant style. In January, he won the Sorrento Cup for the fourth time. At Victoria, in the same month, he set a new course record of 66 for the course now lengthened by about one hundred yards. Back Spin in the *Referee*, always a fan of Harry's, carried the story with headlines, Williams Smashes Another Record. His 66 had not been a fluke for the day before, in a practice round, he had whizzed around in 67.

Over March and April, Harry was in contention in club events and in May was in brilliant form. In a Saturday par competition, he won it with five up with a round of 67. Because of his form, his handicap at Victoria was reduced by two strokes to plus four. Late in May, Harry was invited to play in a mixed foursome exhibition match on the occasion of the opening of the new clubhouse at Yarra Bend. In July, Dick Payne and Harry won the *Australasian* Foursome Golf Shield, Harry, *the most conspicuous player of the four*. The *Australasian* devoted a page of photographs to the event showing, in particular, the large crowds following the final. Harry continued his good play and regained the title of Club champion at Victoria in early August.

The scene was set for another round in the competition between Harry Williams and Jim Ferrier. Their names had been bracketed together since their match before the 1931 national championship. They still carried great power. Golf journalists had their opinion on who was the better golfer. Every golf journalist, when searching for copy, knew that the saga of Ferrier and Williams had legs. It always excited discussion. Now, the rivalry was revived for Jim Ferrier announced his intention to play in the Victorian Amateur title.

Five years before, it had been the common bond of both being sixteen that had intrigued contemporaries. Both were now twenty-one and represented very different golfing paths. Jack Dillon commented that *through periods of intense interest in the game, and occasional lethargy, Williams has been for five years one of the most colourful and brilliant figures that Australian links have known.* By contrast, Ferrier had pursued a more deliberate path to golfing success. He had lessons to improve his swing and worked assiduously to establish this as basic to his golf. He found work as a journalist that kept him informed and influential in the field. He was prepared to interrupt his daily routines to travel overseas for six months for experience. It was now considered that *since 1931, when Williams was the more convincing player, Ferrier has gone considerably further ahead.* In terms of his work ethic, Jim Ferrier appeared the obvious choice to win any contest with Harry.

The biggest crowd ever to attend a Victorian Foursom Championship turned out at Royal Melbourne on the last Saturday in August 1936 to see the young men provide the thrills. Mainly, they wanted to see Jim Ferrier *shoot the works* and next, they hoped Harry would also *fire up*. Ferrier was paired with John Baillieu, also recently returned from England where he had played in the Oxford golf team against Cambridge in 1935 and had participated in the major British championships. They were the hot favourites. Harry with Dick Payne was the other fancied pair. A stiff easterly was blowing and, Ivo Whitton, aged forty-two and Mick Ryan, aged thirty-nine, *experienced campaigners in all conditions*, won the event.

Harry left nothing to chance. He continued to practice. Back Spin of the *Referee* observed Harry at work, *Williams certainly deserves success. I noticed him at Victoria club on Friday afternoon practising assiduously from 4 p.m. until dark. A cold, bleak wind was blowing so strongly as to frighten all but the most hardy off the course; but Harry remained pitching and pitching until lack of light forced him in.* Such a report appeared to contradict the stories of a lackadaisical Harry Williams. Certainly, Harry knew the value of working on his skills. At home, he set up a putting contraption on the lounge room floor for practice. The stories referred more to Harry's motivation to perform at his best. In 1936, the proposed clash with Jim Ferrier was sufficient impetus.

Interest centred on the 1936 Victorian Amateur title at Royal Melbourne in which Jim Ferrier had entered. It was first time that the qualifying stroke rounds were discarded and the title decided by match play throughout. Harry played Jim Ferrier in the third round and the largest weekday gallery every gathered in Victoria each paid 2/6 to watch. In the match, Harry played great golf and it was a conclusive win, he *won almost as he liked.* Perhaps Ferrier had had too much golf or perhaps he had a touch of the 'flu. Perhaps it was Ferrier's putting, normally his best feature, that had faltered. Rather, it was decided, it had been Harry's approach shots that had won this game. Both long and short, they were more accurate, frequently leaving him a single putt. As well, Ferrier's new swing, under the pressure of play, returned to old habits that marred his accuracy.

The result, however, was on the board. They had now met five times - the exhibition game, twice in interstate matches and twice in championships and on each occasion Harry had won. In the final, against Mick Ryan, Harry was five up at lunch and ended up winning on the 33rd in the afternoon, giving Harry the Victorian Amateur title for the third year in a row.

When the dust settled on the 1936 championships, the press passed their verdict on the relative merits of Harry and Jim Ferrier. Jack Dillon in the *Sporting Globe*, was adamant, *we have not in Australia, amateur or professional, a superior to Harry Williams*. Gus Jackson in *Table Talk* was also flattering and raised again the next step for Harry as Britain. *Most good judges are now convinced that Harry Williams is the best golfer Australia has at the moment, and that if he has soon a chance of going abroad he will reach the class of the world's best*. Similarly, *Golf* carried a tribute to Harry's success. *If Harry does not get a chance abroad shortly it will be most regrettable. Undoubtedly he is the Bradman of our golf.*

Harry may have smiled wryly at the metaphor but he was pleased with his continued success against Jim Ferrier. Of all the men he played, it was really only Jim who ever stirred a competitive impulse. Recognising that he was not achieving his own goals usually motivated Harry. After an indifferent nine holes or a particularly disastrous hole, he could pull himself up and address the ball and the course with renewed purpose. His matches were littered by holes he conceded which were then followed by impeccable play. Harry found that competitors, who enjoyed playing against another player such as Ivo Whitton and Mick Ryan, used the stymie to improve their chances on the green. Harry rarely introduced the stymie although, at times, he was happy to benefit from it when it occurred. Harry was not attuned to motivating himself by using the opponent as the catalyst.

At the time, those who observed golf as part of the Australian sporting scene welcomed Harry's outlook on golf. The journalists who tried to present an angle on Harry were often disappointed. In the end, they decided that it was his straightforward manner that was the key to his golf. In September 1936, the *Herald* carried a story on Harry entitled, No Superstitions. *The contrast of Ferrier in his check trousers, and new jade green pull-over, and Williams, in a brown jumper of uncertain age, and ordinary slack greys, led me to ask Williams if the brown jumper was a superstition.* The answer was in the negative but on pursuing the question of superstition, the journalist did elicit a fondness for his 4-wood. On the fairway, Harry used the 4-wood in preference to a more appropriate 2-wood whenever the lie on the fairway was *not so good* and even when the lie was *not so bad*. There was a chink, after all, in his detached calm.

Jim Ferrier never appreciated Harry's approach to golf. It was said that he even hated Harry for his apparent indifference to the sport. For Ferrier, loving the sport meant dedication, being competitive, even aggressive, and chasing opportunities rather than waiting for them to appear. In the personal contests, he adopted all the competitive hints he knew. As Harry was not overawed by Ferrier's achievements, he considered it was only Jim's dedication to putting that was the basis of his success, he was confident about the outcome of their encounters.

Back Spin in the *Referee* was well aware of the tactics and approaches of the two players. In reporting Harry's win in the Australian Amateur championship he wrote, *Ferrier tried new tactics in this game. It was evident he was going to take time, oceans of it. It did not worry Williams. Lately the Victorian has taken to smoking, and while Big Jim was going backwards and forwards and lining up putts and bunker shots, Harry was puffing at his cigarette or performing a rather humorous characteristic of his. It is this: He walks up to his ball and, while waiting for the opponent to play, starts to walk round the ball somewhat like a hen proud of the egg it has laid. And all the time he is whistling softly and concentrating on the next shot to be played.* Harry won that round.

14

To contemporaries, Harry always appeared unruffled, even casual, the study of nonchalance. In 1936, as a twenty year old with plenty of money his was not the life of an Aussie battler. Yet, around him flowed eddies of drama and anxieties. In pursuing his own career, Harry was not always sure of the best path to take. Eric was no longer there to supervise his affairs. Although his mother knew the social scene, she was not interested in golf as a serious pursuit with broadening horizons.

In February 1936, Doll turned forty-three although she did not publicise this. Where her mother would have retreated into black for the rest of her life, Doll had not withdrawn from public life as a grieving widow. She was left a sufficient life income to expect to lead an easy life and she was still relatively young and physically fit to enjoy it. But Doll was often lonely. She had been a caring mother but now, with no demands on her, she had few domestic pastimes to absorb her hours. Harry was no homebody and when she didn't see him for what seemed to her an excessive period of time, she could build herself into a torrent of resentment imagining him to be carefree and indifferent to her needs. The pet terrier was good company but Binkie was not the complete answer to her plight.

Doll liked society; she liked to be out and about, going to the pictures, going away for a weekend to the Grand Pacific Hotel at Lorne or to friends at Portarlington, always waiting for something to happen. She could command Harry to a certain degree to be in attendance. She could talk to Queenie or Eileen on the phone most days. She could go round to Head Street as there was always something happening, on weekends the house would be full of young people. She could ask Eileen to go with her on an excursion.

She could also follow Harry each time he played golf. Indeed, when there was a championship in progress, Doll's days were full and happy. Golf brought out Melbourne society. It was a suitable place to be seen. When Hersey Brookes and Millicent Cairnes, two of Melbourne's most sought after debutantes, joined the gallery Doll enjoyed their company. After the day's play at a tournament, Doll could go out with Harry and his friends and their wives. Golfers mixed with celebrities. Through Harry, she had met Patti Morgan, who went on to pursue a film career with J. Arthur Rank in London. Harry, too, had enjoyed a stint on radio but, it was thought he spoke too fast, and his career was only brief. Altogether, Harry as a golfer, playing on the local courses delivered Doll her most pleasing experiences.

In July, Harry turned twenty-one and on gaining his majority, came into half the assets his father had left in his will. Earlier, in May 1936, Mary Williams, Harry's paternal grandmother had died. Her husband had left her a life interest in shares and investments and a building in Elizabeth Street to pass to Eric and Thelma on her death. It was assumed that Eric's share - estimated at £16,300 in 1928 - now passed to Harry. Harry was suitably impressed. It confirmed his understanding of himself as an amateur golfer with the finances to follow a social life without having to depend too heavily on income from an occupation in insurance.

Yet in 1936, the combination of a loving mother, a considerable inheritance and a reputation as a top amateur golfer limited rather than expanded Harry's options. Late in August, Gene Sarazen returned to Australia for another tour for he had been invited as the major drawcard for the South Australian Centenary golf tournament. In the period since his last visit in 1934, Sarazen had gone on to greater triumphs; in 1935, he completed a grand slam of majors. During the final round at the Masters at Augusta, Sarazen played one of those memorable shots of golfing legend. On the par five 15th, he holed a 4-wood from 200 yards for an albatross.

In 1934, when Gene Sarazen visited Australia, Harry met him but their paths had not crossed to a major extent. It was different in 1936.

Sarazen, accompanied by Helen Hicks opened their tour in Sydney. Sarazen arrived as a world authority and any word he expressed about courses, equipment or players was taken as gospel. His golfing partnership, therefore, with Helen Hicks was taken as an expression of his approval of women players. She, as much as Sarazen, was to be the attraction. In the United States, Hicks was called *hard-hitting Helen* and, to make the point, she played with the men from the championship tees. In an interview, Hicks admitted she turned professional because *having no inclination for the social side of golf, she felt dissatisfied with life after drifting from one big meeting to another, and so made golf her life work.* Since then, she had been employed by sports firms and sports-clothes stores to give exhibition matches and after the matches to advise the galleries on the subject of dress.

The two golfers dispensed large glossy photographs of themselves and were photographed in glamorous poses, more like Hollywood film stars than golfers. They were celebrities and the press followed every move with interest: Sarazen's Gift to Governor, Miss Hicks Rides a Bicycle, Hornabrook Invited by Sarazen to Tour United States Next Year. Whatever they touched turned to news. Gene, his wife Mary and Helen Hicks were also keen on the social life – Helen was reported as saying, *I know how to relax too* - and liked to kick on after golf to local nightspots.

The status accorded to Helen Hicks by Gene Sarazen and hence by his hosts challenged existing notions of the place of women on the golf course. In Australia, golf was a very male world and women were part of it at their discretion. Harry preferred to go to the races on the days when mixed foursome events were played at Victoria, although he was always gallant as a partner. For instance, in May of 1936, when he was invited to partner Leslie Bailey in an exhibition match at Yarra Bend on the occasion of the opening of the clubhouse, he was quite happy to do so but it was hardly a proper game. Indeed, at Victoria, mixed foursomes were regarded primarily as an event for husbands and wives and brothers and their sisters. Hugh Anderson in his column, Down the Fairway in the *Argus* stated as undeniable, *Few men enjoy mixed foursomes, and, frequently play only for duty's sake.*

The culture of the clubhouse, too, was male-oriented. Doll, for instance, had to negotiate a careful path. Women were as keen spectators as men in the gallery but in the clubhouse, Doll found there were parts where she was not welcome. Later in the decade, an *Argus* feature on Victoria Golf Club described it, *Victoria is still a man's club in the fullest sense of the word.* The men's lounge, a palatial room with its leather armchairs and Chesterfields was obviously off-limits.

Then, there was all the business accompanying a round - where the golfers practised and organised their clubs and caddies. Doll found that a woman was certainly not accepted there. As for the men's locker-room, this was a sanctum from which issued stories of practical jokes and personal exchanges, but which was absolutely out of bounds. A huge area occupying the whole of the downstairs at Victoria, there were lockers, baths and showers, a towel room, a drying room, a steward's room, a large bar and bar store, a visiting professionals' room and the professionals' workshop.

Helen Hicks sailed blithely through the visit. Early in September, Sarazen and Hicks arrived in Melbourne by express en route for Adelaide and the South Australian Centenary tournament. Their first appearance at a luncheon as guests of Kingston Heath Golf Club to be followed by an exhibition golf match against Mick Ryan and Jim Ferrier was eagerly awaited. About 2,000 turned up to see the visitors. Neither Sarazen nor Hicks had seen the course before and Sarazen had a round of 73 and Hicks of 82. They defeated Ryan and Ferrier, one up and took to the publicity happily.

The next week, a smaller gallery of about six hundred was at Commonwealth to follow a match between Sarazen and Hicks and Harry and Bill Edgar. The visitors won but the game was played in a relaxed fashion. On the 13th, Bill Edgar borrowed Sarazen's 2-wood to play his second but sliced badly. When Sarazen took it back, he commented *I had better teach that club better habits* and slammed down a long one into the wind that covered the pin. Although spoken in jest, the others were full of admiration for Sarazen's supremacy. But Sarazen was also watching his partners.

Sarazen was on the lookout for potential players for the US circuit, which had developed in the 1920s. In the United States, the top professional golfers earned good incomes, supported by sporting firms, appearance fees and hospitality. Teams of Australian professionals travelled to the United States regularly to compete in events, Ted and George Naismith had recently returned. But Sarazen was also alert to the attraction of a player like Harry who was a left-hander with a flawless swing. That would draw crowds of left-handers who, Sarazen thought, required a model who played left-handed with confidence.

After the game, they were in the clubhouse having a drink and Sarazen began to talk of Harry's golf. *Boy*, he announced to the audience, *he's the greatest hitter of a golf ball I've every seen.*
Then he spoke enthusiastically to Harry, *Why don't you turn pro. and come on the circuit with me? We could play a series of exhibitions and then you could demonstrate for the left-handers and I could take the right-handers. With your great left-handed swing, we could*

show people that this game can be played from the other side of the ball.

Harry looked surprised but when he didn't leap at the suggestion, Sarazen continued,

If you'll come to America with me, I'll make you the richest left-hander in the world.

That would be nice, assented Harry.

I'm talking of a contract and a figure of $100,000 - in your money that's a great deal.

I'll think about it, Harry promised.

The offer was the talk of golfing circles. Bill Edgar, who had been sitting at the table after the game with Harry and Gene and Mary Sarazen, was sure Harry had rejected the offer. According to Bill's memory of the day, he commented to Sarazen, *I think you can forget about it. Either he gives you a decision on the spot, or you can forget all about it.* Edgar was correct. From a boy of few words, Harry had become a young man with a reputation of being brief and to the point. If Harry had nothing he felt would add to the conversation he kept quiet. With Sarazen's offer, Harry could see it only as dislocating his world rather than expanding his horizons and, consequently, his response was muted.

Doll was certainly not enthusiastic. She did not want Harry to leave her to live in the United States. She was lonely now, how could he possibly consider such a proposal. If Harry went to the United States with Sarazen, he would have to become a professional. How could he do that? And if he did, he could never come back to Australian and play as an amateur. Doll indulged in some melodrama and even threatened suicide. Probably, Doll had no need to be excessive in her anxiety to maintain her life as she knew it. She was accurate, however, in her assessment that such a move would completely change Harry's life.

At the time, the decision for a top amateur to turn professional was not an easy one to make nor was the move from top amateur to professional ranks an easy task. It took an exceptional individual to break the conventions. The way into professional ranks still depended heavily on apprenticeships and patronage. For instance, Eric Cremin, who was to dominate professional ranks in the late 1930s, began golf as a caddie at Kensington. There, he won the caddie championship and Mr Harry Hattersley Snr for whom he carried, obtained for him a position with Willie McKenzie at Kensington. It was said, that Hattersley *has in a notable manner had him under his wing all along.*

At the same time, the appearance of Norman Von Nida on the golfing scene offered a different profile for professional golf in Australia. Norman Von Nida, born in 1914, grew up in Brisbane and began as a caddie at Royal Brisbane Golf Club, winning the Caddies' Cup four times. In 1930, when Walter Hagen and Joe Kirkwood played in Brisbane on their tour through eastern Australia, he acted as Hagen's caddie. Von Nida received £5 for his services and an appreciation of Hagen's approach to golf. When Norman Von Nida's father lost his job in the Depression, Norman left school to earn money to help support the family of seven children. He landed work in the state abbatoirs, beginning at 6.30 a.m., and devoted himself to golf every afternoon.

In 1932, Von Nida won the Queensland Amateur championship and was runner-up in the Queensland Open. Norman Von Nida later recounted how at the time he overheard a comment in the club house by a member that they thought it a pity that a caddie should be playing in the final. There was no future for Norman Von Nida as an amateur golfer and he gained employment as a professional at Nudgee Golf Club. However, because he had not served an apprenticeship, the Queensland PGA did not accept him. In 1935, Von Nida moved to Sydney where he established himself as a professional and, more specifically, as a tournament player.

131

But, the income from a professional golf career was limited and Von Nida took every opportunity to increase his earnings. In 1936, when Gene Sarazen came to Australia, a match between him and Von Nida brought wide publicity. Sarazen agreed to play a match with Von Nida, each putting up £50. More than 3,000 people followed the match, which Von Nida won. Other initiatives, such as playing for stakes with professional punters who were also handy golfers and arranging challenges kept Von Nida in the news. In a story on him in May 1936 in *Truth,* Von Nida was already an established identity. Described as *a mighty atom,* stories of his indomitable spirit appealed to Australian ideas of the battler. But then, Von Nida, was not just someone struggling on the margins of society. By his extrovert clothes and entrepreneurial approach to golf, Von Nida created a new style for professional golf in Australia and pushed the boundaries of the understanding of playing the sport.

In 1936, for Harry to consider moving into professional ranks proposed a major change in his view of golf. He was no Norman Von Nida. He was secure within the world of the amateur golfer. He had no first-hand knowledge of the situation for professionals in the US and even with Sarazen to act as his guide, Harry was apprehensive. With Doll actively against the proposal, his comfortable situation in Melbourne and the difficulties such a step entailed, there was no powerful reason why he should accept. Certainly, the amount of money he could earn there was attractive. But he would be playing amongst strangers and in a foreign land, for to Harry, the United States was as alien as any European country.

In golfing circles, Sarazen's flattering comments on Harry's golf made headlines in the daily newspapers. Harry's rejection of the offer and, especially the lure of thousands of dollars, was often discussed. Frequently, these conversations were more like fairy tales, casting Gene Sarazen as the fairy godfather offering Prince Harry the glittering prize of a life of wealth and success on the fabled golf courses of America. Harry was probably more accurate in his assessment that behind the romance of the proposal was hard reality and it was not a step he could readily take in 1936.

Sarazen and Hicks returned to Melbourne for the Australian championships in late September at Metropolitan. Harry was playing well. He had won the Victoria Golf Club Championship and just the week before the national titles he won the Peninsula tournament. With Dick Payne, he won the Australian Amateur Foursome Championship that opened the national titles. In the Open, Sarazen started odds on favourite. The first round began in a furious wind and biting hail. Thus, the first round leaders - Sarazen with 70, Harry Hattersley 70 and Harry Williams 73 - were considered admirable. On the second day, these three consolidated their lead: Sarazen 71, Harry Hattersley 69 and Harry Williams also 69. As yet, Harry was not in the desired groove of his swing so he had had to work for his figures. The third round again produced excellent scores from the top three players - Gene Sarazen 70, Harry Williams 71 and Harry Hattersley 74. By now the aggregate scores were Sarazen 211, Williams 213 and Hattersley 213.

The scene was set for an exciting final round. When the players went out that evening, Helen Hicks was especially attentive to Harry, making sure that he was well supplied with alcohol - *getting him drunk*, according to Doll - and presenting him with a signed photograph of herself. Doll reported all this to Queenie and they decided that it was a plot to put Harry off his game the next day. On the Saturday, Gene Sarazen, playing tremendous golf went out in 35 and home with 36 to post a 71 and a record 282 for the tournament. Meanwhile, Harry went out in 39 - cries of *he's crashed* could be heard from the gallery and Doll and Queenie exchanged significant looks - but then Harry returned in 34, giving him 73 and an aggregate of 286, the lowest amateur score ever achieved in the event. Harry Hattersley came in third.

That night, at the final party, Gene Sarazen talked earnestly with Harry about the possibilities in the United States. Harry listened patiently but the issue was settled. Harry pinned his hopes on the proposed visit of an Australian amateur team to Britain.

15

When Gene Sarazen and Helen Hicks finally departed Australia at the end of 1936, Harry was not left devastated by his lost opportunity. He was a top amateur golfer and in 1937 an amateur team to visit Britain was to be formed. In December 1936 the abdication of Edward VIII and the accession of George VI occupied the conversations around the dining tables of Melbourne. London was still the centre of the world and Britain the home of all things of value. Harry could look forward to taking his golfing career further there. But again, and crucially, the conditions that created Harry as an elite amateur golfer also conspired to limit his opportunities.

The culture of club golf, the home of amateurism in the 1930s, upheld ideas of a golfing tradition in the mould of the Royal and Ancient. It was intensely loyal. In January 1936, when King George V died, Victoria Golf Club cancelled the Monthly Medal competition and the clubhouse and course were closed for the funeral on the Tuesday. It was respectable. At the time, newspapers reported on changes to the dress code taking place in the US towards a more casual style. In April 1937, Hugh Anderson in the *Argus* commented on men's fashions, noting that slacks had largely superseded plus fours. He alluded to the increasing wearing of shorts in Sydney and on northern golf courses although in Melbourne, *several well-known clubs have banned shorts*. Then he recounted the story of how the secretary at Metropolitan was in heated discussion with a member who was refusing to change into respectable long trousers before going out to play, when the Governor's car stopped beside them. Out stepped Lord Somers clad in a pair of shorts. The matter was dropped.

At times, Harry, as a serious golfer, resisted the social demands of this world. Harry's main mentor in golf, Dick Payne, was a good clubman at Victoria and used his influence to support him there. Yet, late in September 1935, Harry Culliton in the *Australasian* had the news that Harry was about to resign his membership at Victoria and become a member at Kingston Heath. Back Spin in the *Referee* also carried the story, reporting Harry as saying of Kingston Heath, *Never have I played on a better or more testing golf course, nor one that was better prepared for a championship.* He was persuaded not to move and, in 1936, played consistently at Victoria and represented the Club in pennant.

Nevertheless, in 1937, Harry's approach to club golf appeared to be dismissive. The cause lay in his lifestyle. He may not have sought the more formal social conventions of the golf club but Harry saw golf as blending easily with a sociable life. After the Australian championships in October 1936, Harry relaxed from the demands of championship golf. It was reported that *mostly he has been content to enjoy a game with his friends*. Often, these friends were drawn from Harry's other main interest, horse racing, and took him away from the manoeuvrings of elite golf.

By now, Harry's interest in racing was well established and a tale that was often repeated whenever this was mentioned highlighted his growing preference for the excitement of racing rather than for golf. At Victoria, Harry was playing off plus four in the Saturday afternoon par competition that meant he owed a shot at both the third and the sixth holes. Harry was also keen to see the main race at Caulfield that day. He eagled both the 3rd and the 6th and birdied six of the other seven holes so that he was eight up at the turn. Harry decided to go. He marked the back nine down as nine losses for a net score of one down, signed his card and off he went. It was said that he won the event as well as getting to the races on time.

Although the story came to vary in its details, the substance remained. Some said that Harry set out to play the first nine in convincing style so he could leave for the races; others, that the idea only arose after the first nine. Some said that Harry had not won the event on the day. Others said that Harry went into the clubhouse for a drink and decided to stay and listen to the races on the wireless for the rest of the afternoon. But all agreed that Harry's aims in golf were not those of an ambitious man. Harry's command of the skills of golf was such that he had only to turn the switch and they leapt into life. Equally, he could walk away from a record round. That the objective was not to win some competition but to indulge in the more romantic Australian passion for horse racing was also considered significant. It was not the action of a prudent businessman.

In 1937, it also became apparent that, without the requirements of top golfing events enforcing personal rules of moderation, Harry slipped into the habits of heavier drinking. Whereas most of Melbourne suffered the closure of pubs at 6 p.m. and all day Sunday, golf clubs provided a haven for their members. The loophole that alcohol could be served on Sundays with meals saw members sitting up in the dining room, ostensibly eating a meal, but primarily enjoying a glass of beer or whisky. Alternatively, members could keep alcohol in their lockers and when the bar was closed avail themselves of their own supplies.

Although Club Councils and Directors might issue edicts, members ignored them and alcohol was an essential part of the day's and evening's activities. Joe Johnson, in his history of Royal Melbourne, told of the judges who were members there, sitting with their backs to the bar after hours so they would not be obviously involved. Sir James Macfarlan, however, justice of the Supreme Court and known for his irascibility on the bench, preferred to be more open about breaking the law and drank with other members at the bar.

By the late 1930s, Harry's drinking was no longer dismissed as the exuberance of youth or the usual accompaniment to social occasions. Doll, who had been worried about Harry's first experiments with alcohol, was concerned. She nagged him and made excuses for him. From members of the club, there had been a range of responses from jocular acceptance to veiled criticism. Throughout, though, Harry was watched closely and his drinking habits discussed. At different times, it was reported that Harry was drinking at lunch, between rounds as well as after rounds, that he kept alcohol in his locker. Confidentially, word circulated that Harry was *drinking*. In this, he was no different from countless other golfers but, for Harry, performing at the highest level in golf these irregularities carried greater penalties.

Generally, Harry rested on his reputation for most of 1937. In March, he captained the Victoria team that went on to win the Pennant. During the Easter period, Harry played in two exhibition matches with Dick Payne and then with Mick Ryan against Joe Kirkwood and Walter Hagen who had returned for another tour of Australia. A gallery of about four hundred watched the latter game.

For the rest of the 1937 season, Harry re-appeared only for the *Australasian* Foursome Golf Shield and for the Victoria Club championship. In both, his form was poor and reports of his play were littered with adverse comment on all aspects of his play. He had *missed a yard putt, driven out of bounds, had another bad drive, found the bunker, took four to reach the green, three putted for a shocking seven, put in another poor round* or *was out of touch*. He was also criticised for not playing fighting golf, *One feels that Harry Williams is sometimes over-generous in giving away holes when a brilliant recovery, of which he is certainly capable, might save the day.* Needless to say, Harry did not carry off either title.

Late in July, Jack Dillon, normally a great fan of Harry's, represented him as an enigma, *despite many magnificent efforts, he appears to be unconvincing at times*. He continued: *there comes every now and again a lackadaisical attitude*. Dillon concluded that Harry needed some impetus, *It takes something to make him put his mind on his golf*. Two weeks later, Dillon reported that Harry was still playing erratic golf, mixing *brilliant play in private games where a few balls have been at stake with some stuff not quite worthy of his undoubted great ability*. Dillon proffered Harry's explanation: *his own translation of his variegated form is that he is finding some difficulty in getting down to serious consideration*.

The Australian championships were to be held at The Australian in 1937 and Hugh Anderson, late in August in the *Argus,* stated his view that he considered Harry out of the running for the forthcoming championships. *A few months ago I would have added Harry Williams's name ... but recently his golf has been of such an uncertain nature that his name cannot be added to the list of probables*. Doll, worried that Harry's new golfing partners were in her words, *bad company*, tackled him as he was driving her home from an outing one Sunday. Harry had learned long ago to ride out his mother's anxieties by silence and now he concentrated on the road and let her criticisms flow over him. Not that Doll was hostile or condemned him for his lapses but she wanted him to maintain his place in amateur golf and its culture where she also found a pleasant space.

By September, Harry was in Sydney for the 1937 Australian championships, not as yet swinging perfectly but getting there. Indeed, in the interstate game, when Jim Ferrier played Harry, he finally broke Harry's hold on their contests and for the first time won. Although the press recognised the success, this event was not awarded much significance. Commentators considered Harry, at that point, was not competitive. The next week, headlines announced, H. L. Williams Back to Best Form and Back Spin in the *Referee*, commented that over the period, Harry had *converted a game from hopelessly sick* to championship golf.

The 1937 championships were particularly important for Harry. It was thought that the amateur team to go to England in 1938 would be picked from the successful golfers at the national championship due to commence on Thursday 9 September. There was discussion about who would impress. Two of the professionals, Reg Jupp and Jock Young discussed the field for the Open on the Wednesday evening:

Norman Von Nida has had a meteoric rise. This could be his big breakthrough. He appears the most tuned-up, capable, confident and physically fit man in the field. He is a better golfer now than he was a year ago. But in the showdown with Billy Bolger, Bolger outplayed him and took the £50. So, you'd say Billy Bolger is hot at the moment, reasoned Jock Young.

Take it from me, Ferrier will win this championship, replied Reg Jupp. *The big tearaway can score so well with wild golf, and everyone knows that he can play really amazing shots. He has played so much since he was a mere kid, has been so tremendously keen, and has packed so much experience into his six or seven years of big golf, that I reckon he is as mature and as case hardened as any of the men in the field.*

Jock Young broke in, *Williams could rise to the occasion. He runs hot and cold and I hear that he's not doing much at the moment, that he's down on form. But when he gets going, he can gather up the birdies too. I hear he's had a lessons with Bill Clifford here in Sydney and then a round with Charlie Conners which will put him right. And so far he's shown he can outplay Ferrier when he's in form. Then, of the rest of the amateurs, there's Hattersley. He's improved a lot and he's probably at the peak of his golf. I'd say there's about five in contention.* Jock Young numbered them off, *Billy Bolger, Norman Von Nida, Harry Hattersley, Harry Williams and Jim Ferrier, four of them from New South Wales.*

Reg Jupp returned to his favourite,

In the NSW close championship of a couple of years ago at Killara and again the year after at Manly, Ferrier didn't just beat par in one sizzling round, nor even murdered it, he massacred it. And everyone knows the big fellow is the best putter we have seen in this country.

I thought I knew a lot of things about golf, Jock Young concluded, *and many times it has had me wondering. But the one thing that I still feel for a fact about it is that if you want to know the winner of a championship, the only safe place to find out is on the scoreboard.* They both laughed and agreed to compare notes at the end of the championship.

The championship was at Kensington. After work on The Australian course, the golfers agreed that the fairways were well covered, the greens were in good shape, the rough was fair but not by any means drastic and the remodelling work and bunkering had been well designed and admirably worked out. At most holes it was possible to be considerably off line from the tee and yet get home and secure par. It was still not considered as difficult as Metropolitan, Kingston Heath or Seaton but more testing and difficult than Rose Bay. On the second day, however, when a northerly gale swept the links, lashing the sand from bunkers and sending clouds of sand over the course, players found it hard going. Only thirty players in the field of one hundred and seventy managed to break eighty. George Naismith won the event, the relatively high score of 299 attributed to the difficult conditions.

In the 1937 Australian Amateur championship that followed the Open, Harry hit form. In the second round match, Harry holed twenty pars and five birdies in the thirty holes he and Frank Headlam played and on the 415-yard 14th, drove within fifty yards of the pin. In the final, despite Tom Tanner's grim fight, Harry never looked like losing. There were dazzling pitch shots, superb bunker shots and crashing drives. There was a great eagle: on the 545 yards 22nd hole Harry split the fairway with a great drive and then from the hill sent a 3-iron to fifteen feet of the pin sinking the putt for an eagle three. Tom Tanner stayed in the game for Harry tired and held on to his lead to win narrowly. *It was only recovery work of a brilliant sort after drives sent off the line, approaches played with an art, finish and sense of how to grip a ball and just how much to give it and the most persuasive touch on the greens that saw Williams through.*

With this victory, observers were convinced that Harry proved he was a *class* golfer. For the range of his game and for persevering when he was obviously tired, Harry was now termed *a grand fighter*. Hector Morrison in the *Daily Telegraph* considered that Harry took out the title *with flying colors as a sportsman and a great golfer*. H.W.S. in the *Sydney Mail* gave Harry further accolades. Harry was pictured as *the finest amateur in Australia.* Moreover, H.W.S. considered that Harry and Eric Cremin, who won the professional championship, had come through *with the knowledge that in all ways they had lived up to the best traditions of the game. And the game is the thing.* Harry had, it appeared, confirmed his place in the team for England.

16

For the whole of Harry's playing career, playing golf in Britain had beckoned as the closest approximation to Paradise. As soon as Harry had won a major title, the question of not whether he would go overseas but when he would go was before him. In 1937, the Australian Golf Union formed a sub-committee - Ivo Whitton, Robert Nettlefold and Charles Rundle - to select an amateur team to go to Britain in 1938. The team was to spend six months away. It seemed that the opportunity had arrived.

The Australian Golf Union, as the pre-eminent governing body for golf in Australia, exercised added power as the only Australian administrative body affiliated to the Royal and Ancient Golf Club in Scotland. It was considered, therefore, a most august body made up of representatives of the *five favoured* clubs, those with championship courses, and the six State governing bodies. The AGU set the main dates of the golf calendar and deliberated on the rules of the game. The Australian Professional Golfers' Association also set a calendar of events. From the viewpoint of the AGU, professional tournaments were seen more as providing a livelihood for players and were not to be seen as the showcase of Australian golf. Primarily, the AGU interpreted Australian golf as an amateur sport.

As selection in the team was the highest accolade that could be bestowed on an Australian golfer by the AGU, choosing an amateur team for Britain was an important task. In the press, various criteria were put forward to provide an objective basis for selection. Most often the view was expressed that the team would consist of the best golfers. After all, this

143

was an opportunity to display the Australian golfers to the wider world. Attention might also be given to young golfers, ones who would learn most from the experience and come back and raise the standard of Australian golf. Perhaps it would have representatives from each Australian state.

But these suggestions had to be reconciled with the understanding of the meaning of the amateur golfer in the late 1930s. The financial status of the amateur was apparently clear cut. The amateur could not profit from the game. And, of course, the team would not include a player where there was the least suspicion that he had done anything that even in a minor way could be construed as offending the amateur definition.

Rumours of possible infringements proliferated in golfing circles. For instance, Ivo Whitton published *Golf by Whitton*. It was a best seller, selling 90,000 copies. It was thought, however, that this compromised his amateur status and publication stopped. He was profiting from the playing of golf by writing a book on the sport. Arguments for and against appeared to be arbitrary for benefiting from the sport was very open to interpretation.

If amateurs should not profit from the game, should they incur a loss? To make the trip golfers had to be absent from Australia six months. By the 1930s, amateurs were generally not those who wrote 'gentleman' on a form when their occupation was requested. A trip to England could pose financial difficulties. Someone with a family and in an occupation where they were unable to get leave of absence might not have the money to go. Harry was the exception rather than the rule in enjoying an independent income. At the time, it was estimated that more than half the top amateur golfers in Melbourne had come into golf from caddying, indicating a less privileged pathway to club golf.

Bill Higgins, who came to prominence with his win in the Victorian Amateur title in 1937 had at the age of fourteen served as a caddie to members of the Metropolitan Golf Club. Born in 1913, Bill's father had urged him to play every sport he could and, in doing this, he had to learn the hard lesson of *how to take a hiding*. He joined the Oakleigh Cycling Club and then for a year and a half he was a boxer and played for Oakleigh Football Club. On the road and in the ring, he gave and took some hard knocks. In the early 1930s he'd gone to the country timber cutting but in 1934 returned and took up golf seriously, winning the Caddie championship. He then found work in the motor trade and joined Kingswood Golf Club, then at Dandenong. Having just established himself after the privations of Depression, Higgins was hardly in a position to leave for six months overseas.

More open to interpretation was the understanding of the character of the amateur. Early in July, the matter was aired in the columns of the *Sporting Globe*. The team had to be composed of players *who by their personalities and bearing will be a credit to Australia*. This was particularly important *by reason of the fact that the team will, while abroad, be the guests of golf's most famous and exclusive club*. The observer indicated that this condition had implications for individual golfers in Australia at that time: *There are unfortunately, even among our most talented young amateurs, odd ones whose lacks in this respect would make the selectors wary about naming them.*

Of course, there was speculation as to which golfers this referred and the nature of their misdemeanours. Back Spin in the *Referee* evidently found it necessary to address this criteria on behalf of Harry. After asserting that Williams Should Be In Amateur Team For Great Britain because he was an Outstanding Golfer And Fine Personality, Back Spin elaborated on some of talents of which the selectors may not have been aware. *I have heard him make a couple of very nice and surprisingly sensible speeches. Opinion is growing too that despite some things to the contrary, he is really a nice lad, sensible, courteous and a thorough sportsman.* Indeed, Harry was *a surprise packet* who would *do credit to Australia.*

By September, the sub-committee made it known that their ideas of representation related to a broader definition of golf than a rank order of merit. They announced that in selecting four players and a manager, they were considering the goodwill and ambassadorial side of the individuals and the team more than the playing ability. No one will be sent, it was stated, *who is not rated a type who will on and off the links fit in with the high standards associated with British golf, and particularly with the circles in which the team will be moving.* They also announced that the players named would have to undergo a medical examination before their selection was confirmed.

Again speculation was rife. Such an emphasis on goodwill questioned the nature of the visit. Evidently, the English organisers, fearing a continuation of *bodyline*, wished to place the emphasis on matches of a friendly nature. If individuals were good enough to be members of leading clubs and to compete in national championships, why wouldn't they play amicably in Britain? If there were men medically unfit to take their places, why hadn't the state or national governing bodies picked it up and taken appropriate action before this? Talk about the *best types* was also seen as a double standard. If men were playing golf in Australia who were not suitable, why was this tolerated? In other words, none of these conditions precluded the sending of a team of the best players.

During the Australian championships in Sydney, talk centred on the selection and opinion still held to merit as the main criteria. The golfers, who had performed well, it was thought, would have to be assured selection for the team to go to England. Defining the best golfer at any

146

time occupied hours of discussion. Now, Jack Dillon in the *Sporting Globe* grasped the nettle and took the unprecedented step of naming his top ten golfers from both amateurs and professionals. Jack Dillon explained his list. Personal details, he stated, had not been permitted to intrude. Besides performances in play and competition, consideration had been given to the methods of shot making, the temperaments, the personalities and other points considered to have a bearing on playing golf.

From the amateurs, they were, in order: H. Williams (Vic), J. Ferrier (NSW), H. Hattersley (NSW), T. McKay (NSW), D. Davies (NSW), L. Nettlefold (Tas), A. Rae (Vic), M. Ryan (Vic), L. Duffy (Vic), S. Keane (Q) and from the professionals: N. Von Nida (NSW), V. Richardson (NSW), W. Bolger (NSW), G. Naismith (Vic), E. Cremin (NSW), J. Waler (Q), C. Booth (NSW), F. McMahon (SA), E. Naismith (Vic), R. Stewart (SA).

Pointing to the difficulties of reconciling the two types of golfer - the amateur and the professional - Jack Dillon stated that he had intended to include amateurs and professionals in the one list. But, he continued, *No matter how I tried I was not able to do this in a manner that carried conviction to myself.* He did, however, consider it possible to name the four best golfers in Australia at the time. They were 1. H.L. Williams. 2. N. Von Nida. 3. J. Ferrier. 4. V.S. Richardson.

For Harry, one immediate factor clouded selection. This was the factor of physical fitness. At the Australian championships Harry complained of a pain in his groin to Doll. By the end of the tournament and his final against Tom Tanner, Harry was getting very tired and sat down whenever possible. At first, he had thought it was only a muscle strain and expected it to come right by itself. It didn't, and Harry thought it must be a torn muscle. Although Doll murmured sombrely of some internal sickness to

Bill Higgins's mother who was in the gallery with her, the pain was diagnosed as a hernia. It didn't hurt except if Harry did a sudden sharp twist or if he played a lot of golf. It was not catastrophic but it would not heal itself and would require a minor operation.

In the middle of October, the sub-committee called Harry for a medical examination as part of the process of selection. Harry fronted up for his appointment. When the doctor examining him asked whether he had any problems, Harry told him he had a hernia. The doctor completed the examination. A few days later, Harry was called into the sub-committee again. They told him they had received the report of the medical examination and that he had a hernia. Harry acknowledged this. But then, they informed him that, to comply with their requirements, he would have to have an operation for the hernia at once, in the next week or two or else he wouldn't be selected.

Harry was surprised. *But that's out of the question*, he said. *I'm willing to have an operation but the doctor says that it is not severe and immediate action isn't necessary.* Ivo Whitton, Robert Nettlefold and Charles Rundle were not sympathetic. Harry, for once was upset and angry. He would get another opinion. When Harry met the specialist, he assured him that an operation in January would be fine and that he would be fit and well to depart with the team. Harry went back to the sub-committee with the news. They, however, would not hear of any change. The decision had to be made. They couldn't take the chance of him breaking down on the tour.

By now, Harry recognised the situation. Speaking to the three men, he realised that they would not be moved, that basically they did not want him on the trip. Doll, without this knowledge of the body language that had been expressed during the exchange, wanted to take it further. *I'll go and talk to them myself*, she offered.

148

It's no use, they've made up their minds they don't want me.
I'll ring up Jack and get him to attack them in his column.
The decision's been made. They know it's going to cause talk but
they can say I'm medically not fit.
But that's not right, fumed Doll. *There's no better specialist than Mr*
McDonald in Australia. If he says a January operation is fine, it is.
Backwards and forwards, and round and round. Each time, though,
Harry came back to the cold hard fact that he had been rejected.

The Victorian Amateur titles in 1937 began early in November and Harry
was physically fit to play. He started as straight out favourite for the
event but was far from keen about competing; it was said he was *short
of practice and out of form.* He arrived half an hour late for his first
round because he had trouble starting his car. Without even a preliminary
swing, he proceeded to play good golf to beat Bill Wishart in the first
round. He just got by in the second round against Alex King in a hard-
fought match. In the next round, Harry did not play well but still won. In
the quarter final, Harry played Hugh Hamilton, who had already eliminated
Mick Ryan. Harry lost the match on the 18th when Hamilton drove it
and birdied the hole. Bill Higgins beat Dick Payne for the title.

The team was announced in mid-November, a fortnight after the Victorian
Amateur titles. It comprised: H. W. Hattersley (NSW), T.S. McKay
(NSW), L. Nettlefold (Tas) captain and M.J. Ryan (Vic) with Sloan
Morpeth (Vic) manager. There was uproar. Harry was missing and also
Jim Ferrier.

Because those named were each most commendable, criticism of the
selection largely centred on the claims for Harry and Ferrier for inclusion.
Jim Ferrier's exclusion made the headlines. Social Snobbery, shouted
the headlines when officials of the Manly Club, where Ferrier was a
member, were asked their opinion. On the weekend of the

announcement, Jim Ferrier defeated Harry Hattersley in a match decisively, by seven with five to play. But it was Harry's omission that created most comment. Back Spin in the *Referee* considered it lacked confidence in Australian golf. *Perhaps it would not be so hard on Ferrier, for he was abroad only recently, but it would seem a great pity if Britain were not permitted to see a player who, in the opinion of no less an authority than Gene Sarazen, is the greatest left-hander in the world.* Through the 1930s, Harry Williams shone as the brightest star on the Australian golf scene. On the occasions when its isolation had been broken by visiting celebrities, Harry had been singled out for commendation. He was a golfer of world standing. A team without him was not in the interests of the sport.

In the gossip surrounding the news, attention moved to Harry's role in the course of events. Harry was consulted. Back Spin reported that *a well-known golfer rang to say that Harry wasn't keen to go in any case. Thought I'd check up. 'I'd like to go, all right,' said Williams. 'There's nothing I'd like better.' So that's that.* The impression that Doll may not have wanted Harry to make the trip was also squashed. Jack Dillon quoted Doll's reaction to the news, *Mrs Williams, Harry's mother, a well-known figure on the links of three States, was bitterly disappointed at the unfair treatment she said had been meted out to her son.*

On the part of Harry, Dillon evidently responded to criticisms of Harry's behaviour for he addressed this aspect of Harry's golf as if it were at issue. For six years, he stated, he had followed him in the major events, and almost always had stayed at the same hotel. Harry's manner and his manners on the links had been impeccable. Regarding Jim Ferrier, Dillon referred to allegations that his amateur status was in doubt. Ferrier's regular column in the *Sydney Morning Herald*, it was suggested, might be interpreted as financial gain. However, Dillon warned that Ferrier had no opportunity to refute the claims and should be seen as innocent until proved otherwise.

Just to show how gracious Harry Williams was in defeat, Jack Dillon invited him to write a column in the *Sporting Globe* on the team selected. Publicly, Harry was relaxed about the decision, *There were certain conditions laid down by those selecting the team. I did not conform to one of those conditions. That's all there is to it.* Harry regretted Ferrier's absence and praised each of the men selected although he did point out that Len Nettlefold had not won a major event since 1928, nine years before.

Some columnists immediately moved in to support the selected team. Hugh Anderson, in the *Argus* of Monday 15 November, defended the process of selection. He also observed that alternative plans to open a fund to send Harry and Jim Ferrier to Britain independently would jeopardise their amateur status. By Friday's column, Anderson was smoothing over the divisions the selection of the team had caused. He concluded that the team was, after all, *a jolly good selection* and that as neither Ferrier nor Williams were *wholly trustworthy* in their golf, they may not have been successful anyway. Indeed, *Williams would have had a better chance, perhaps, if he could arouse himself sufficiently to reach the form he showed in the 1936 Open championship*. Such reasoning begged the question of the performance of the others selected but drew attention, in a suitably veiled manner, to concerns about Harry's personal life.

That Harry had just won the Australian Amateur title that year should have automatically gained him selection. However, Harry became a victim basically because his private life was not considered appropriate for an amateur. In the end, the hernia, itself was of minor importance in Harry's general physical condition. Doll had developed a medical history of Harry as firstly a delicate child, given to asthma, and now added an internal problem to his afflictions. But dealing with the hernia did not interrupt Harry's golf to any extent.

In 1935 and again in 1937, golfing columns carried reports of Harry's health as relevant to his golf. No other golfer earned the same attention. Doll might elaborate an unfortunate medical history as an alternative explanation of erratic play. Harry's regular caddie, Brian Stegley, might be extra solicitous in supporting Harry during a round. Journalists might ascribe *poor health* to Harry's lack of interest in golf and playing partners might contribute to a myth of Harry's performance under the influence. They were all allusions to the impact of drinking on Harry's life.

Harry's golfing career was at times interrupted by periods when drinking broke the demanding patterns of practice and playing required for consistent performance at the elite level. Probably, too, Harry began to feel he could not function effectively without the stimulus of alcohol. However, in personal terms, moral condemnation in the form of exclusion from the amateur team was hardly the best prescription for the disease.

17

After the announcement of the selection of the amateur team at the end of 1937, Harry turned his back on the world of club golf. He absented himself from Victoria Golf Club seeking a more genial environment. In the enviable position of being financially independent, Harry was in a position to pursue any interest that he found gave him pleasure. Golf, as he had to play it, did not always fulfil that role. Without a professional or a commercial occupation, Harry became part of the more amorphous but still powerful male culture centred on alcohol, gambling and the race track. At the end of 1937, Harry sought refuge in its sociable networks.

Harry had nurtured an interest in following the horses as part of the repertoire of a young sporting male. Going to the races and following the racing calendar provided him with an agreeable social milieu. By attending the races, Harry could meet people or keep to himself, have a drink, have a bet, all in a culturally sanctioned space. It was a constant kaleidoscope of people, through which Harry picked his own path.

An afternoon at the races was as structured as Harry made it. At Caulfield, there were three distinct areas - the flat, the paddock and the guineas – each with its own crowd. Harry preferred the guineas though sometimes he went to the paddock to meet up with someone. On his arrival, Harry might reconnoitre the crowd to find out the current gossip but decide his first plunge would be on a tip from his barber - that Aurie's Star has come back from Sydney where it didn't do well but should do better today at Caulfield. Then he might fall in with an owner of the horse that had won the last race who, in an expansive mood, insisted on taking him to the bar for a celebratory drink. There, they could miss the next race as others joined them and on the advice of someone, who had it from the jockey, Harry could take in the saddling enclosure and survey the field on his way to the ring. Although the totalizator had been introduced on Melbourne courses in 1931, Harry preferred betting with the bookies. Amongst the hundreds operating, he bet with a couple who knew him well and he always headed purposefully through the crush to place his bet.

Then, Harry might head for a seat in the grandstand to watch the race. There were numerous acquaintances who might put him in the way of a *good thing*, at very short odds but definitely *the go*. After consulting the form he might decide to take the advice. The race begins; his heart beats faster, the favourite takes an inordinate amount of time to run down the outsider. Afterwards, they repair to the bar to down a whisky before collecting their winnings. With variations, sometimes spending more time in the bar, sometimes outlaying larger amounts, sometimes winning more than losing, sometimes losing much more than winning, the races offered Harry a satisfying social world.

At the races, Harry met and, for a time, paid attention to a young woman of a family who would have most satisfactorily met Doll's strict criteria. Her father, however, declared that Harry drank too much while Harry thought the future father-in-law was one of the most illiterate men he'd every met. The young woman did not even get to be taken home to meet Doll. Instead, she married another suitor and became a formidable, titled matron on the Melbourne social scene.

Harry found the racing fraternity congenial. Their lifestyle was good. They drove good cars. They ate well, drank well. Money didn't seem to be a problem. They moved between the cities of southeastern Australia easily. When Harry was with them, he met all sorts of people. They were like a family. The bookies asked after the wives and families of the jockeys, the trainers inquired of the bookie's day at the recent meeting.

Everyone knew each other. In May 1938, the racing world and Harry, in particular, was shocked by the death of two jockeys in an accident at Morphettville, the worst in South Australian racing history. One of the jockeys, Ray Wilson, aged twenty-eight, was a good friend of Harry's. When The Leader fell, Trimercian, ridden by Wilson, came down over it and Wilson was killed when he struck his head against one of the posts of the running rail. Ray lived in Miriam Street, Caulfield, a stone's throw from the racecourse and Harry was a regular visitor. Harry often followed the horses Wilson rode especially when he was on the three-year-old Hua. The day it won the VRC St Leger at Flemington, Harry remembered fondly for he'd had a good collect.

In racing circles, Harry was accepted as a gambler. In the culture of racing, gamblers were important figures for it was their enthusiasm that fuelled the industry. At the racecourse, the gambler earned respect. There were the big gamblers like Eric Connolly or Jack Heeney but there were also the gamblers who brought a certain style to the ring. On Melbourne courses, there was Miss Pearce elegantly dressed and betting in £100's, the boxer hat man who was short in stature but impressive with a boxer hat and a very large wad of cash and then the striking John Woolcott Forbes, in spats and with a flower in his coat lapel. In the crowds at the races every Saturday, such figures promenading through the ring were dramatic characters and, like the bookies, added to the spectacle.

But gambling was not just a race track event. After World War I, horse racing boomed and the introduction of the wireless in the mid- 1920s further expanded the audience for the sport. Even the *Women's Weekly* carried a regular feature, Betty Gee's 'Racey' Narratives. However, as only on-course gambling was legal, the individual wanting to have a bet on the races but unable to attend was forced to find alternative means. Starting Price bookies, operating as a network of individuals providing a service attached to hotels, sporting clubs, barber's shops and billiard rooms around the city or a telephone service for those who had a phone, were, by the late 1930s, an institution. As it was illegal, SP bookies were not invited openly into hotels and clubs and like after-hours drinking, such betting was condoned but not officially sanctioned.

Golf clubs were lively spots for SP betting and Harry was an enthusiast. Many members were involved with racing, from owning to training to riding. Although off-course betting was illegal, it was an interest a golfer was expected to display. By the 1930s, the wireless, with its race commentary, was a focus of attention on race days and commentators like Eric Welch had established the race call as an art form. Members would give the head steward their bets to put on for them or more often the professional shop would be the centre of the betting. They would ring up and get the odds and then they would ring up five minutes later and get an up-date so as to keep members informed. It was a part of club life.

Wagering, generally, had been connected with golf from the outset. Horace Hutchinson in 1890, in his classic volume on *Golf* produced for the Badminton Library, asserted that, in golf, *the normal man will not exert himself without the inducement of a bet*. Indeed, *we fear the game would languish if the harmless and necessary half-crown were by law forbidden*.

As golf became more popular and the standard of play improved, the introduction of organised competition - pennant, state and national championships - established an alternative purpose to playing. Indeed, golf shared with other sports organised in the late nineteenth century, the impulse to translate physical endeavour into outcomes favouring merit and verifiable achievement as ends in themselves. However, gambling remained an integral part of the golf scene.

Golfers established stakes for a game. It might be a ball out, a ball in and another two on the match. This was customary. But, occasionally in the press, a note of protest would be sounded. In January 1938, Hugh Anderson in the *Argus* found it necessary to sound a warning about *the growing evil of heavy wagering in matches*, betting in pounds rather than in golf balls. Anderson had recently heard of two young players who had won nearly £100 in four matches. He also reported watching a match in which one of the players was losing more than £250 at the 15th hole. Although these particular players could afford to lose the money, Anderson considered them to be a bad example to younger golfers.

Harry, a top player, was a likely candidate for a wager. He had money and confidence in his ability. There were plenty of players looking to hazard their luck on the golf course. As there was largely Saturday racing - about twice a month there was a racing on a Wednesday at either Ballarat or Bendigo - those involved in the racing industry were big users of the golf courses during the week. Indeed, Woodlands Golf Club, which adjoined Epsom race course and was also close to Mentone race course, was regarded as a club where jockeys, trainers, owners and bookmakers predominated. By 1938, Harry was evidently part of this circle for the rumour was that he had joined Woodlands Golf Club, to consolidate his association with the racing fraternity.

There was so much doing if you were a gambler in Melbourne, in the late 1930s. Monday, Wednesday and Saturday nights there were the dogs, Friday and Saturday nights, the fights. Then Saturday races - the three major metropolitan courses - Caulfield, Flemington, Moonee Valley - or maybe Mentone or Williamstown. The bikes at North Essendon. A country meeting every so often. Cards on Sunday night. Billiards at Lindrum's in Flinders Lane. About half a dozen baccarat schools operating in the city - in Elizabeth, Lonsdale and Exhibitions streets. The gaming was largely organised by men with criminal backgrounds but they made sure there was no trouble for the common interest was the gambling.

This was a male world and Harry found that relaxing. Generally, it was away from the emotional demands placed on him by his mother. Of Harry's age group, of those born in 1915 in Australia, only 2% were married by the time they were 20 in 1935 and only 32% by the time they were 25 in 1940. By the age of 30, 70.5% were married. This was part of a trend towards more people marrying and marriages taking place at an earlier age. In 1935, for instance, of 30 year olds only 59% were married whereas those born in that year, by the time they were 30 years old, in 1965, 79% were married. There was plenty of company for Harry of other men who were not committed to going home to wife and family.

The edges of this world were blurred. The races gave some work for a large number of people - the bookies themselves, clerks, bagmen, touts, tipsters, urgers. For the rest of the week, though, most had to find other work. In Melbourne, the wharves were the biggest employer of unskilled labour and many combined work there with the race track. The wharves also enjoyed a similar culture as the racetrack - one where income was based on a daily selection for employment meaning either money in the pocket or none. There were periods of slack when the form guide offered the best read. The racing and gambling culture also flourished in city gymnasiums and billiard halls where men came together in a social setting.

Because gaming and off-course betting were illegal, they existed in a quasi-criminal environment. According to the newspapers, gaming took place in *dens* and was labelled *vice* in headlines of police raids. Police raids on SP bookies were more constant. There were so many operating that rarely a week went by without a report of a raid in the newspapers.

The SP and the gaming school could be intimidated. Protection rackets, where an SP bookie was approached with the recommendation that his patch required defending or stand-over tactics, employed to push an SP bookie out of business, were organised by men with criminal records. Then, if apprehended and questioned as to their means of support, they found that registration on the wharves as a painter and docker gave them a legitimate occupation without requiring substantiation. The wharves were again linked with this cultural scene that flourished in Melbourne without official sanction.

All operated within a social setting lubricated by liquor and characterised by late nights. Restrictions on drinking remained severe. In 1938, there was a determined effort by a number of interests, including the Temperance Alliance, to introduce prohibition to Melbourne. The vote was decidedly against abolition but hotels continued to close at 6 p.m. The Melbourne institution of the six o'clock swill, when men jammed into the austere tiled bars to line up glasses of foaming luminous amber was something Harry tried to avoid. He preferred the more relaxed surrounds of the golf club, his local hotel out of the peak hour and the different bars of the more up-market city hotels like Scotts and the Australia in Collins Street.

After-hours drinking, like gaming, was available even though it was illegal. Often there was entry for the regular patron at hotels around the city and many sporting clubs made their profits from after-hours trading. There were also a few nightspots where alcohol was available but as with gaming, in a clandestine manner. At the time, for instance, Joyce Walker, the daughter of a Victoria Golf Club member converted the old Victoria Golf clubhouse on the original Sandridge site into a nightclub - The Spider Web. Don Walker had been a champion cyclist and apart from playing golf at Victoria ran the Sandridge Golf Club after Victoria had moved to Cheltenham. A nit keeper kept a lookout for potential raids by the police as the clientele drank at their leisure. Similar establishments persevered in providing nightlife to the metropolis, always illicit and often shoddy in the hard light of day.

As with his drinking, rumours of Harry's betting circulated around golfing circles. Some said he gambled big sums, others that his wagers were more modest. Some said he was lucky and was a winner, others that he was losing heavily. In many instances, the interpretation of Harry's gambling rested on the speaker's appreciation of Harry himself. Doll was particularly critical of Harry's friends, rarely varying from her assessment of them as *bad company*. Harry's gambling certainly did not improve his financial position and neither Doll nor Harry developed strategies to augment their income by other means.

But Australian golf generally and Victorian golf in particular missed Harry. As Back Spin in the Referee concluded his review of 1937 that it was regrettable Harry had been seen so little. *To the 'galleryite' the champion left-hander is always worth travelling several miles to see. Big golf in this State seems a little flat without Harry's presence.* In April, 1938 Harry played his first game for many months when a friend enticed him to Metropolitan in order to film him. Jack Parker, the film maker, reported that Harry's golf *was not his best*. He played only ten holes and his hands were so soft that he rubbed a patch of skin from each thumb. He had put on weight, and in July, was thirteen stone. Normally, Harry was described as a tall slender young man so this transformation was quite surprising.

If Harry was moving away from the Victoria Golf Club in a cultural sense, he remained sufficiently committed to playing golf at the highest level to return to the Club at the time of the championships. At the board meeting at Victoria on 28 July 1938, Harry's membership was discussed for Harry had not paid his dues for 1937-8 or for the present year. The Directors had also heard that he had joined Woodlands. He was sent a letter and Dick Payne asked to talk with him. On the 28 September, Harry presented himself at Victoria to meet the directors and personally apologised for his actions and applied for re-admission as a junior member.

On the motion of Bob Weir, seconded by Joe Carrigan, he was again admitted as a member.

Although Harry returned to Victoria Golf Club in 1938 and entered into the round of championships and matches, this was no longer the only way in which he thought about the game. He knew he had the ability to take on anyone but now he had to set rules on his behaviour so as to continue to play the game at the highest level. Sometimes, however, he broke his own rules.

In early August, Harry re-applied himself to the business of preparing for a major event and he was seen practising putting and bunker shots in a systematic manner. This change of mind was greeted with approval. Back Spin in the *Referee* voiced his satisfaction. *It has seemed all wrong that such a brilliant exponent of shot-making should have his clubs stored away in the hall cupboard.* When the 1938 Australian championships began in mid August at Royal Adelaide, Harry was there.

Playing in the Amateur Foursome Championship with Dick Payne, the pair had a sparkling 73 in the morning with steady, consistent golf, but then, in the afternoon they failed. For such an experienced pair, the failure was remarkable and, of the two, Harry was said to be *playing the less convincing golf.*

Jim Ferrier, writing his regular column in the newspapers, added his observations. *I cannot recall a similar happening in a national championship in the past few years.* The sub-heading, Williams Inconsistent, was followed by a comment on Harry's play, *Williams was in a spasmodic mood yesterday, playing some brilliant shots, but then following them with loose hitting.* Some attributed the transformation to a long lunch although others remarked that Harry had been *turned out to grass for twelve months* and could not be expected to return to big golf so suddenly.

When the 1938 Australian Open started, Harry began with a round of 80, *hitting the ball all over the place and putting badly*. For his second round, he had a score of 73 in which he took forty putts. Jim Ferrier had a record 68 on this second round but then Harry equalled that with a magnificent third round. Harry was out in 34 and seemed certain to be home in 33 when his solitary miss-hit of the round, a cut second wood at the 17th, went into the rough. On the final round, Harry, suffering from a severe nose bleed, scored a commendable 78 and finished tied for fourth. Jim Ferrier went on to win the Open from Norman Von Nida.

In the Australian Amateur championship that followed the Open, Legh Winser eliminated Harry in the first round of match play fairly easily. Playing with a plug in one nostril in the morning, he was severely handicapped. Jim Ferrier, the defending amateur champion, went on to win the Amateur title, defeating Dick Payne in the final.

It was Jim Ferrier's tournament. What he and Harry had in common was further eroded. Jim Ferrier had married in the January of that year and took his wife to the tournaments as symbol of his adult status. With his regular columns on golf in the *Sydney Morning Herald,* Ferrier was now an authority on the sport in Australia. His columns were studded with personal references for Ferrier also spoke as the leading amateur golfer of Australia. And now, Ferrier's double victory was a major achievement.

Harry's erratic form continued. When he returned to Victoria, Harry played in the 1938 Victorian Amateur championship. In the second round there was a sensation. Tom Gardiner, a Kingston Heath junior, beat Harry narrowly. Bill Edgar won the title. Yet, Harry could not be dismissed as a spent force. At the end of the year, he was selected to play two exhibition matches with the visiting Bobby Locke and, again, praise for his golf from this eminent golfer recognised Harry as an exemplary golfer.

162

The first match between Bobby Locke and Harry was at Bendigo. The course was dry and hard and there was a strong wind. Locke finished the outward round in 38 to be two up but Harry was square at the 14th. Over the last four holes, Locke drew away to win, two up. Observers admired Locke's long and accurate driving, his longest being about 340 yards. The second match was on the first Sunday in December at Kew, when Harry and Dick Payne played Locke and Willie Smith, the Kew professional. Locke and Smith won the match, one up. Bobby Locke revived Sarazen's praise for Harry's golf. Locke said that Harry was the finest amateur *hitter of a golf ball* he had seen, and he would like to see him have encouragement with a trip overseas, where *he would rival the best amateurs in the game*.

If Harry's behaviour had caused his rejection from the amateur tour for Britain, he now confirmed it by declining to be part of the regular round of club events. By identifying with the racetrack rather than the Royal and Ancient, Harry made a quantum shift in cultural terms. Although Harry remained a young man of social standing, in Melbourne, in the late 1930s, the racing and gambling world merged into the notorious. It was not clear what Harry's role in this was in 1938 but to contemporaries it was a departure from accepted conventions of the amateur golfer, to be treated with a degree of awe but largely with scepticism.

Nevertheless, while the development of interests outside golf made an impact, Harry remained a principal golfer on the Australian scene. Even though his golf was inconsistent at the major championships, Harry had still finished tied for fourth in the Australian Open and his third round of 68 at Seaton was a marvel of power and control.

18

It was only in hindsight that 1939 emerged as the end of both an era and a decade for Australia and for Harry. In January, the worst bushfires in Victoria's history coined the term Black Friday but remained only a threat on the horizon to suburban Melbourne. Similarly, the photographs on the front pages of the newspapers of worried men in hats and overcoats hurrying to meetings in London or Berlin appeared remote.

In the back pages, racing and football, and columns devoted to sundry other sports showed a city enthusiastically going about its weekly routines. On other pages, large advertisements for Dining Settings, seventeen guineas; Three Piece Lounge Suites, sixteen guineas; and Player Pianos, £95; inserted by furniture stores like Maples, Clauscens and Pattersons (the firm with a million friends) indicated the lifting of the strict economies practised earlier in the decade.

On the golfing scene, familiar themes appeared in new forms. In 1939, the appointment of Charlie Conners as professional at the Victoria Golf Club placed the occupation of the golf professional under renewed scrutiny and occupied many hours of meetings and discussion over the winter months. The Professional Golf Association, showing concern for its authority as a professional body, objected to the appointment for various reasons. The Victoria Golf Club eventually won the ensuring battle and Charlie Conners was accepted as Club professional. The case, however, did indicate that the Professional Golf Association was very watchful of their right to control their own ranks. Although Conners won the case and held his appointment, he resigned soon after because he stated there was not sufficient income from the position.

Australia continued to be an important destination for American golfers. In June, Babe Didrikson arrived with her husband George Zaharias for an exhibition tour of Australia, she to provide the spectacle of a powerful woman golfer and he to wrestle. Her drives of 260 and 300 yards evoked cries of *colossal* from the gallery. At the beginning of July, Babe Didrikson came to Melbourne and began the visit by playing a private exhibition game at Victoria with Charlie Conners. It was a performance. Her husband, acting as caddie, played the clown to her straight role as golfer. But even then, he reassured the audience, *Remember, she's only a girl*. Early in August, Babe Didrikson entered the Australian Open to be held at Royal Melbourne but the match committee rejected her application. The reasons were not specified and did not refer to gender as an issue. However, Australian golf was certainly not ready for that sort of equality, even if her golf was *marvellous, just marvellous*.

Harry, too, returned to the familiar program of the golfing calendar but 1939 saw several departures from previous routines. Harry was now working as a traveller for a Melbourne firm and, it was thought, this gave a better structure to his life and golf. By 1939, Harry had been playing top golf for ten years although he was still comparatively young, turning twenty-four during the year. With this depth of experience and his undoubted talents, Harry reasserted his presence amongst the winners. There was another episode in the series of meetings between Harry and Jim Ferrier and, late in the year, Harry again confronted the hoary chestnut of his amateur status when he attempted to broaden his golfing horizons. In 1939, too, Dick Payne announced his engagement to Betty Bolton.

In July, the Victoria Golf Club championship became a contest between Harry and Dick Payne. Harry began his last round with a lead of six strokes over Dick and although he had a mediocre 80, he won with three strokes to spare. Jack Dillon in the *Sporting Globe* was pleased to see Harry back in golf commented, *Williams does not get over enthusiastic about his golf, but was genuinely pleased about the way he was hitting the ball*.

In July, too, Harry and Dick Payne, representing the Victoria Club won the *Australasian* Foursome Shield held on the East Course at Royal Melbourne. The weather was wet and windy, the fairways and greens were sodden and there was casual water everywhere. Prominent amongst the spectators was Doll who attracted the attention of the writer covering the event. While others sheltered beneath umbrellas, Doll, in her white mackintosh, red gloves, socks and bag, led the gallery throughout, the rain dripping from her hair. At the end, she strode through the fierce sleety shower to the clubhouse, to greet and congratulate *her boy* and Dick and then, at last, to seek shelter.

In the last week of August, the 1939 Australian championships were played at Royal Melbourne. For the first time, a West Australian team competed in the interstate competition held before the main events. The team of Harry, Laurie Duffy, Bill Edgar, Dick Payne, Bill Higgins, Mick Ryan and Alex Rae in that order first defeated New South Wales and then Western Australia in the final. Victoria also won the professional match.

In the Open, Harry had rounds of 75 and 74 and then in the third round played a dazzling 32 home for a 70. Although this score included a seven, Harry played superb golf - *the stuff only Williams at his best can play*. There was a particular sequence of holes that dazzled the crowd. Starting at the par five 12th, Harry slammed his second shot, a 4-wood to five feet of the pin and put it down for an eagle three. After a perfect pitch to the 13th green, he putted a twelve footer for a two and a birdie; a par at the 14th, and then a drive, a glorious 4-wood and putt of eight feet for a birdie at the 15th.

And so it went, Harry performing the miracle of immaculate golf. However, Harry's final round of 73 left him in sixth place with Jim Ferrier first, successfully defending his title.

The Australian Amateur title followed with Jim Ferrier also in the field. In the championship, Harry played some great golf. In the quarter final, he met Alan Waterson, the New South Wales amateur champion and after the morning round, Waterson led by three holes. In the afternoon, Harry picked up on the 28th in disgust when his third fell short of the green. Then on the 29th, his frown changed to a broad grin when he holed a sixty-foot putt from the edge for a three. At the 36th, the match was square. The big gallery rushed to watch the 37th. Harry's second reached the green and he putted for a three and a win. In the semi-finals, Harry played Dick Payne. In the morning he started very uncertainly and was six down after the eighth hole. By the eighth hole in the afternoon, however, the match was square and then Harry pulled away and won easily.

The final between Jim Ferrier and Harry Williams was promoted as yet another bout in their struggle for recognition as the better player. In the morning, play was close. Harry caused a buzz of surprise in the gallery when he pitched fifteen foot past the hole on the 10th, did not hole the putt and then conceded the hole, letting Jim Ferrier off a putt of a yard. This was a habit of Harry's, conceding putts that were not necessarily 'gimmes', and, given that Jim Ferrier had earlier missed a putt of that length, this was considered to be too sporting by half.

Harry finished the morning one down but in the afternoon, now playing to a gallery of 2,000, Ferrier played very accurately whereas Harry played many great shots but made mistakes from which he did not recover successfully. On the 22nd and the 29th, ending up in trees, he declared the balls unplayable and conceded the holes. Throughout the afternoon, amateur photographers in the gallery constantly interrupted Harry and he frequently had to ask the referee, Sloan Morpeth, to have it stopped so he could take his shot. On the 25th, the intrusion was clearly evident when Harry took three putts from the edge of the green and lost the hole. Jim Ferrier won the match convincingly.

At the conclusion, Ferrier, The Wolf, was gracious in victory, claiming, *Harry is a great golfer. He is a natural player, wonderfully gifted. I am not that gifted. It is hard work that gets me any good results that come along. Harry has got that grand swing of his. Mine is different. He should turn professional. If that boy simply had to play golf he would be a wonder. If his bread and butter depended on it you would not see the others for dust*. That aside, Ferrier was all talk of his and his wife's departure for the US where he intended to play in the major events.

On September 3, Australia following Britain's lead, declared war on Germany. The schedule of golf continued for the time being. On Monday 11 September, playing with Alex Rae, Harry won the Victorian Amateur Foursome Championship at Yarra Yarra with an aggregate of 159 under difficult conditions of rain, hail and high winds. Then in the 1939 Victorian Amateur title, Harry, playing great golf won the early rounds impressively. In the semi-final, he was around in 72 in the morning and was four up on Bill Edgar at lunch, going on in the afternoon to win in convincing fashion, *playing his long game brilliantly*. In the final against Laurie Duffy, playing on his home course at Yarra Yarra, Harry was in championship form - on the edge of the 528 yard 9th in two and, at the 17th, he drove 340 yards. Harry was three up after the morning's play and went on to win the Victorian Amateur championship in the afternoon for the fifth time in nine years.

Even though war had been declared in Europe, Harry's golfing horizons broadened. At this time, Norman Von Nida's schemes brought Harry into their orbit. By the late 1930s, anything Von Nida did, the press seized on. He was always a photographer's opportunity. In 1939 at the Australian championships, when he broke his putter across his knees after three putting on several greens, they were there to photograph him with his new putter and to relay the story with relish. But Von Nida was not just a publicity seeker. He was constantly looking at the entrepreneurial possibilities of golf, arranging challenges, exhibitions and displays of the best Australian golfers for paying spectators. He began to look to the Pacific and Asia for possible venues. In 1937 Von Nida approached Harry to go to the Philippines to play in the rich tournament there in the following January. In the event, Harry did not go but Von Nida did and won the Phillipines Open.

In 1938, Von Nida again approached Harry to join him in an overseas tour and rumours circulated of the plan. To undertake the trip, it was suggested that Harry would have to turn professional. In October, Back Spin in the *Referee* canvassed the pros and cons of Harry's situation. On the one hand, he observed, *Former amateurs do not seem particularly welcome in professional ranks.* On the other hand, amateurs usually regretted their choice. *He has all his pals members of clubs. As a professional he has more or less to renounce them too. He has not the free run of the clubhouses; he can't dine with them, in some clubs he cannot even join them at the 'nineteenth' hole.* When asked directly, Harry replied, *I am remaining an amateur.* He agreed that he might take a trip to Manila or to Britain or America in a couple of years, *but* he said, *in either case it will be as an amateur.*

Just as Dick Payne had continued to support Harry, so Norman Von Nida actively encouraged Harry to remain in the top ranks of Australian golfers. This time, Harry prepared to accompany Von Nida to the Philippines. Harry, as a left-hander was a good attraction. Curiosity over his amateur status continued, especially when Harry announced that he was going to the Philippines for business reasons and a holiday. When asked the whereabouts of Von Nida, Harry replied he was travelling on the same boat. Harry had paid for the fares. To further questions, Harry replied that they may play exhibitions games while they were away. However, Harry did not expect that to infringe his amateur status, as it was an accepted practice in Victoria for amateurs to display their skills in this way.

In the Philippines, the Australians played golf in an oasis of calm and affluence. Talk of Japanese expansion was guarded. Norman Von Nida kept tight control of the trip. Harry was limited to drinking coca-cola. One night, Von Nida heard thuds coming from Harry's room and on going to investigate found Harry standing on his bed, driver in hand, swatting mosquitoes. *Bloody mosquitoes!* Von Nida was reported as remarking that it took an exceptional golfer to swat a mosquito with a driver.

It was a successful foray into the tournament scene, for Harry carried off the Amateur title. However, it was not financially profitable. In 1937, when Jack McLean, the leading British amateur of the 1934 team that visited for the Victorian centenary, turned professional when he announced his engagement to be married, he asserted that, even in Britain, the home of amateur golf, there was no future for him. The costs of playing golf for an amateur were too high. Similarly, while Harry had enjoyed Philippino hospitality and brought back impressive trophies from his tour, this did not convert into pounds and shillings.

The trip was accompanied by increased international tensions. At an official level, the Australian government was unwilling to recognise the militaristic plans of the Japanese government. Strikes in Australia had drawn attention to Japan's continued march across Korea and China and the atrocities accompanying it. Wharfies refused to load pig iron bound for Japan, asserting that it would be used for military purposes. In November 1938, R.G. Menzies, as attorney general, enforced the dog collar act to secure the export of pig iron, earning the nickname Pig Iron Bob in the process. Although uncertain about the intentions of Japan in the Pacific region, the government dispatched the first Australian troops for Europe in January 1940. In August 1940, John Latham was appointed as Australia's first diplomatic representative in Japan.

19

While the excursion to the Philippines broke the usual rhythms of Harry's life, the demands of war now intervened to change them altogether. When Harry returned to Melbourne, the war was beginning to make a greater impact on the life of the city. In March 1940, golf in Melbourne moved into recess, for the next six years, competitive golf was suspended. During this period, Harry moved out of contact with the social networks of club golf that continued in Melbourne and developed a lifestyle that, while satisfying, did not include championship golf.

The ranks of golfers thinned. Both Harry and Dick went off to enlist. For men, brought up on the romance of flying during the decade of the twenties, the air force was an obvious choice. Indeed, when enlistment opened, the airforce was the first of the services to fill its training schools. Dick joined the RAAF, as did Bill Higgins and Norman Von Nida, but Harry's health prevented him taking this path. Harry joined the army but was discharged due to his history of asthma. Doll was relieved although she found she had to make sure people knew of Harry's asthma so as to protect Harry from criticisms of shirking.

There was a major change in the arrangement of Harry's personal life that diverted Doll's focus from Harry and his golfing world. Doll fell in love. At a party, Doll had met Len May. Leonard Emanuel May, born in 1899 to Charles Emanuel and Margaret May, nee Grogan, worked on the wharves as an examiner and tally clerk. He had a steady job and offered Doll the company she had been missing. Doll now officially lowered her age by three years to meet the conventional notion of the husband being the older of a couple. Leonard did not particularly impress

Harry. He was no sportsman and he had no claims to social status. However, Doll was insistent that he should at least tolerate her new husband without overt criticism.

Although Len was not a wharf labourer, the fact that he was associated with the wharves was, to the family, a social misfortune. Doll tried not to tell anyone because the view of wharfies had been coloured by years of sensational media coverage. In their view, wharfies were rough and rude, a thorn in the side of government. They never did a decent day's work and were either on strike or drunk. When telling Queenie her news, Doll kept repeating that Leonard was a good man and that he would look after her. He was still not welcomed with enthusiasm. They were married in a church in Caulfield followed by a reception at Mulgoa Street.

When Doll and Leonard set up their home in Orchard Street, Brighton, they invited Harry to live with them. Although they were comfortable, evidently, Harry no longer considered himself an affluent young man. Whether to recoup monies laid out for himself and Von Nida to go to the Philippines or to pay other debts, several times, after they came back from Manila, Harry rang Von Nida with the story that someone had stolen his clubs. Von Nida, working for Spalding at the time, replaced them for Harry on each occasion.

Harry, Doll and Leonard soon moved from Brighton to Millswyn Street in fashionable South Yarra. Just off Toorak Road, their house fitted between blocks of solid flats built on the subdivisions of the grounds of the mansions that had once extended along St Kilda Road in the nineteenth century. Favoured with names like Millswyn Court or Hawaii Apartments or Ardlui Flats, the area harboured a genteel population. Physicians had their rooms there and music teachers encouraged their pupils through yet another rendition of Marche Militaire or Für Elise. Afternoon tea was still a social event for the Miss Beargates and the Miss Russells who lived in the flats and who might meet at the Poplar Coffee Inn around the corner or buy some chocolate eclairs from Sugar and Spice Cakes to take home to indulge discreetly. At the city end of the street, Harry found the Botanical Hotel in Domain Road a handy local.

In December 1941, with the Japanese bombing of Pearl Harbour, Australia was plunged into the Pacific war and Melbourne became a major centre for American troops. John Curtin had become Prime Minister in October 1941, and now mobilised the nation to meet the crisis. It was compounded in February 1942 when Singapore fell. In March 1942, General MacArthur arrived in Melbourne to take up residence at the Menzies in Collins Street while two hundred and fifty officers occupied the Chevron Hotel. In June, there were 30,000 US troops stationed at sites dotted around the city, including the Melbourne Cricket Ground and Royal Park. The RAAF took over Caulfield racecourse. During 1942, Melbourne moved to a war footing with thousands in the armed forces, employed in munitions or in some way conscripted into the war effort.

At the same time, other measures were introduced to control civilian life. For a while a brownout was in place and yards of trenches were built. Generally street lighting dimmed and shops closed at 6 p.m. People settled into weeks of long working hours, travel restrictions and petrol rationing. Harry was issued with a Manpower identification card, accrediting him as appropriately employed. He was a taxi driver. In June, ration books were issued. Doll found rationing most severe, although their combined allocation was quite satisfactory and Len and Harry's work placed them in positions to access the thriving black market.

Behind the driver's seat, Harry was a frequent observer of the other side of the war, the efforts to maintain morale. In the city, the best fares came

173

from the hotels like Scott's or the Australia Hotel in Collins Street where the officers drank and from the Dug-out, opposite the Town Hall, where Myers and Buckleys provided partners for the troops for supervised dancing. There were less decorous places. There were always fares around Flinders Street when assignations beneath the clocks decided on a destination for the evening. During the war years, seven new cinemas opened in the city. At night, Harry generally kept away from the stretch from Princes Bridge to the Shrine along St Kilda Road and the Alexandra Gardens where couples sought the privacy of darkness. He reasoned the soldiers' wallets were usually empty by the time they called a taxi.

Harry's reputation for being unflappable on the golf course served him in good stead as a taxi driver. In July 1942, the Leonski trial repelled the residents of suburban Melbourne. Harry was asked repeatedly had he picked up Leonski as a fare or perhaps a girl who had escaped his clutches. The trial exposed the extent to which the legal restrictions on drinking and gaming were unobserved in the city. In the wake of the trial, there were attempts to make this a public issue, but to no avail. The social world based on alcohol, gambling and racing that Harry knew from before the war, flourished.

Racing, although scaled down, proceeded as good for morale. It was limited to Flemington and Moonee Valley for Caulfield was out of action and Williamstown closed. In October 1942, the government introduced a raceless Saturday each month but for the rest of the time, racing proceeded. With increased spending power, gambling expanded. Proceeds from the black market could be relayed back into circulation through gambling, providing another impetus. Gaming clubs increased and with them, the demand for alcohol after 6 p.m. Melbourne might still be closed at night and on a Sunday but Harry, driving a taxi, knew a whole string of old and new addresses where clients could find whatever they sought. He could also frequent the same venues.

By contrast, the ties that held Harry to club golf loosened. During the war years, Harry retreated from Victoria Golf Club completely. When the golfers who were still around Melbourne formed themselves into a group called the Oakleigh Boys and organised events in aid of the war effort, Harry was not amongst them, although his caddie, Brian Stegley, later was. In 1941, Harry played in some of the tournaments organised by the association of public golf courses, the Victorian Golf League. In May, he played at Forest Hills and in September, at Patterson River. In the Victorian All-Comers' golf championship at Patterson River Harry, who finished equal second, entered from the Brighton Golf Club. Brighton Golf Club was a public course. In 1936, when it was opened, the dignitary given the honour of hitting the first ball missed it entirely on the first effort and then hit the photographer recording the event with his second. During the year, Harry would have heard that in the US, Jim Ferrier, after some controversy, had turned professional.

Nevertheless, Harry did not turn his back on playing golf. Harry, it was reported, was to be seen on the public courses around Melbourne. As well as Australian players, there were Americans who liked a wager on a game of golf and new stories about Harry Williams began to circulate. The sight of Harry ambling on to the tee, appearing unconcerned by the task ahead, disarmed men who did not know him. Their doubts soon turned to respect as Harry would split the fairway with elegant style.

By 1944, some of the restrictions of the war were lifted. In August, Caulfield re-opened and Harry and Doll and Len were amongst the crowd of 50,000. In November, however, their family circle was broken when Queenie died from a heart attack. Doll was forlorn. Although they had very different approaches to life, they were twins and Doll had depended on Queenie. She had talked with her daily, visited her often and had always sought her out as a sounding board. Doll may not have taken the advice proffered but Queenie had been a sage counsel.

In many ways, Harry, Doll and Len survived the war years relatively successfully. For Len, the normal business on the wharves during the war declined but wartime measures finally rationalised the method of employing men and, generally, the wharves were more efficient. Although there were fewer ships arriving, there was still plenty of activity and at times Len was able to bring home items from the cargoes that were much appreciated by Doll. Silk stockings, unavailable from 1942, occasioned Doll's greatest delight. For Harry, there was perhaps one more opportunity to embark on a life independent of Doll when another romantic interest appeared in his life. Evidently, this association, produced by the conditions of wartime, ended tragically when the woman committed suicide.

VE Day was widely celebrated but it was not until August 1945 that the war in the Pacific ended. Evidence of the war years lingered on in Melbourne life. Rationing that had been introduced during the war was not immediately lifted. Petrol rationing remained until mid-1949 and butter rationing until mid-1950. Energy supplies were often erratic and blackouts were a recurring incovenience. It was not all gloom. In 1948, the first migrants arrived, displaced from their homes and countries by the war but now bringing diversity to Australia's predominant Anglo-Celtic population. At the same time, the first Holden car rolled off the assembly line, evidence of the success of the manufacturing sector's wartime expansion.

In the bright new world of the post-war years, Harry did not pick up the old threads of his life. Dick, who had risen to the rank of Flight Lieutenant and flown as navigator in Marauders and Liberators against the Japanese, returned to a family and suburban domesticity. Norman Von Nida left for England in 1946 to put himself amongst the money-winners on the international circuit. Increasingly, new names, like Ossie Pickworth, Peter Thomson and Doug Bachli, appeared in the headlines of the golfing columns, players Harry had never played with.

In 1950, Dick Payne made an attempt to bring Harry back to club golf. Fred Dawborn, a past captain of Victoria Golf Club and Dick met with Harry and, when asked he agreed that he was keen to return to golf. They arranged a game at Victoria. Playing with a set of left-handed clubs borrowed from Archie Raitt, another member, Harry put in a 71. Fred Dawborn was impressed, *He did it so easily*. Having seen that Harry was still competitive, Dick Payne and Fred Dawborn organised Harry to appear before the club directors, agreeing to meet at Scotts Hotel in Collins Street on the afternoon of the meeting. They met, had a couple of drinks and then Harry, saying he would go home and change, would meet them in the clubhouse at 7.30 p.m. Harry, however, did not turn up. When Fred Dawborn rang him the next day to find why he had not appeared, Harry, somewhat embarrassed, gave what to Fred appeared a lame excuse. Basically, Harry had turned his back on competitive golf and closed that chapter in his life.

If the Williams family had been major participants in the changes following World War I, those that succeeded World War II largely passed them by. The massive immigration schemes initiated in the late 1940s deposited thousands of people from all over Europe in Melbourne. Yet, in South Yarra, Harry, Doll and Len were isolated from this influx. Neither were they recipients of a new flat because their slum cottage was reclaimed. They had no primary school children drinking free milk at recess or lining up for immunization against tuberculosis and whooping cough. They did not participate in the expansion of public secondary education nor was Harry eligible for a returned soldiers' scholarship for tertiary education.

Doll and Harry had always enjoyed a good standard of living and a high level of consumerism. For many in the 1950s, a car was a major event but they had owned cars since World War I. The proliferation of goods in the 1950s introduced them to plastic and vinyl and terylene but did not signify the leap in their standard of living that it did for those who had

177

years of thrift behind them. Television was a novelty, although it did not replace the wireless and the newspaper as their main sources of information. It was not something they eagerly went out to purchase as soon as it appeared.

In this changing society, Harry had neither the existing position nor the skills to give him a sudden jump up the ladder as it did many others. Nor did he have the inclination to seek training in a new field. Instead, Harry found occasional work largely through his social networks, as a penciller for a bookie, as a clerk on the wharves. For Len, meanwhile, the opportunities on the wharves actually decreased. The trend to carrying goods in bulk intensified after the war and, as well, moves to mechanisation transformed work practices. The workforce fell dramatically. Niether Harry nor Len were in a situation to take advantage of the boom of the 1950s expansion.

Yet Harry continued to live well. Doll was particular about keeping the house in order. Their antique furniture may have been considered old-fashioned in the contemporary rush to acquire divans and bar stools but it was still in good taste. Harry and Doll, sometimes with Len and sometimes with Eileen and her husband, continued to go to the races. One time when they were leaving Caulfield with crowds milling around and Eileen recovering from an operation, there was not a taxi in sight. Harry hailed a police car and talked them into driving her home. There may not have been so many invitations to social events but that did not worry Harry.

Generally, Harry developed a reputation as a loner. He had a number of haunts he frequented - Lindrum's Billiard Rooms in Flinders Lane, the local pub, the baccarat school in Lonsdale Street. Although he liked the company at Lindrum's, he rarely played. If someone spoke to him, he'd reply and was quite sociable in that way or if there was a game going on, he would sometimes sponsor a player. But, generally, he kept to himself. Indeed, he went out of his way not to draw attention to himself.

To the hurrying crowds, Harry, appeared as a middle-aged bachelor, displaced by the Depression and war. Those who knew his story pointed Harry out to their friends. But Harry had no interest in publicly re-living his major achievements. He still played golf with a circle of friends. Bill Nicholson remembered picking Harry up at 6 a.m. from a baccarat game and taking him out to Yarra Bend. There, he borrowed clubs from the professional and, after viewing the first fairway rather blearily, settled in to record a par round. To the end of Harry's career, the contradictions of his approach to golf fascinated his contemporaries.

By the end of the 1950s, however, Harry's world narrowed. They moved from South Yarra to Weybridge Street, Canterbury or Surrey Hills, as the area was also known. The new house was cheaper to rent. Doll may have understood the gradual decrease in her buying power but did not want to recognise the unpleasant consequences. Her response was to continue as she always had. Expenditures that in the past had been ordinary became luxuries. Sometimes, it could not be ignored. Eileen was in hospital and received a wonderful bouquet of flowers - roses, gardenias, carnations - it was delightful. It was from Doll, concerned and ready with the thoughtful gift. Eileen left hospital, weeks passed and then she began to find florist's bills in her mail. The florist, tired of getting no response from Doll, was now trying the recipient to pay the bill. Doll's credit was lessening every month.

Death again entered their lives. Len had been in poor health and in 1959 he died. Doll's family may not have seen Len as a suitable second husband for Doll, but his death left a notable gap in her and Harry's daily routines. Dick Payne was diagnosed with cancer, and in September 1960 he also died. Neither Doll with an ulcer nor Harry with asthma complicated by a heavy consumption of alcohol was in robust health. Doll, the life of the party, began to experience periods of depression.

179

In 1961, when the new TABs opened, Doll continued to have a flutter on the horses even though ready cash was an increasingly scarce commodity in her life. Increasingly, Doll's thoughts turned to suicide. In September 1961, she told a friend that if she were to take her life, she had decided that she would use gas. Another day, she announced that she had tried to gas herself but had not been able to go on with it.

At Weybridge Street, Doll and Harry fell behind in their rent. The recession of 1961, coming after years of expansion, appeared disastrous. When 5,000 workers were sacked from Ford and General Motors, there was a sense of shock. To Doll, it appeared they were in the middle of bad times, which were getting worse. If anything happened to her, what would happen to Harry? In her view, he could not look after himself.

Doll and Harry decided to avoid the immediate problem of finding the money to pay the rent at Weybridge Street by moving. Before they packed their belongings for the flat in Hartwood Street, East Kew, Harry and Doll invited Eileen and her husband over to Canterbury. They gave to them a J. B. McDonald oil painting handed down from the Halfey's time of grandeur in the nineteenth century. Harry also gave to them some of his golfing trophies, including several he had won in the Philippines and a framed photograph of the Great Ocean Road presented to him on the occasion of the opening of the Great Ocean Golf Links in October 1936 by His Excellency The Governor, Lord Huntingfield, KCMG. Then they moved house.

On the night of Tuesday 12 December 1961, Doll and Harry took stock of the situation. They had established only a temporary hold on Hartwood Street, there were three crates of belongings to unpack. They had no money and no prospects. Doll had always lived without compromising her lifestyle. Some argued that even Harry had been sacrificed to her demands. The degree of Harry's involvement was questionable. He was only forty-six. He had not expressed any ideas of suicide previously and now may have been an unknowing partner in Doll's plans. Or he may well have seen the future as bleak, considered this action quite feasible and willingly acquiesced.

At any rate, it was Doll who organised the event. She wrote a note confessing that they could not go on without money and placed it on the kitchen bench. Then she closed the door into the lounge room and carefully crammed feltex in the gap under the door and did the same with the door that led into the garden. Opening the oven door, she turned on the gas and, with Harry and their pet terrier, prepared to quit forever the world they had known.

EPILOGUE

According to the myth the 'typical Australian' is a practical man... He is a great improviser, ever willing 'to have a go' at anything... Though capable of great exertion in an emergency, he normally feels no impulse to work hard without good cause. He ... gambles heavily and often, and drinks deeply on occasion. Though he is 'the world's best confidence man', he is usually taciturn rather than talkative, one who endures stoically rather than one who acts busily. ... He tends to be a rolling stone, highly suspect if he should chance to gather much moss.
    Russel Ward, *The Australian Legend*, 1957

Of course all life is a process of breaking down, but blows that do the dramatic side of the work - the big sudden blows that come, or seem to come, from the outside, the ones you remember and blame things on - and in moments of weakness, tell your friends about, don't show their effect all at once. There is another sort of blow that comes from within - that you don't feel until it's too late to do anything about it, until you realise with finality that in some regard you will never be as good a man again. The first sort seem to happen quick - the second kind happen almost without your knowing it but is realised suddenly indeed.
    F. Scott Fitzgerald, *The Crack-Up*, Esquire, Inc., 1934 and 1936

In 1957, Russel Ward's *Australian Legend* was published. In it, Russel Ward created the immensely influential figure of the typical Australian. In assembling the characteristics of the typical Australian, Ward may well have been thinking of Harry Williams. Born in 1915 in the year of Anzac, Harry's life commenced auspiciously. Like the typical Australian, Harry, in his golf, was *a great improviser, ever willing 'to have a go'*. He was someone who *gambles heavily and often, and drinks deeply on occasion*. He was often described as *taciturn rather than talkative, one who endures stoically rather than one who acts busily*. In working, *though capable of great exertion in an emergency, he normally feels no impulse to work hard without good cause* and in personal relationships Harry was described as a loner, a man who was *independent* and who *tends to be a rolling stone*.

But in 1961, when Harry Williams died in Hartwood Street, East Kew, he was not celebrated as a Chips Rafferty or a Peter Finch who were at that time gracing screens around the country as typical Australians. In many ways, the tragedy of Harry Williams was that the attributes, which Ward defined, as making the Australian male did not always produce the happy ending of the contemporary feature film.

There was no one moment when Harry's life changed irrevocably. As Scott Fitzgerald wrote in 1934 when Harry was already immersed in the good life and good golf, the blows of life *don't show their effect all at once*. But, more seriously, and more far-reaching was the other kind of blow, the one *that comes from within*. These second kinds happen *almost without your knowing it*. So it was with Harry.

When he looked back over his life, Harry resented his father's authoritarian attitude. But many boys in the 1920s suffered a heavily disciplined life. In Harry's case, however, this was combined with a mother's doting on an only son. Socially, this may have restrained Harry from developing as a lighthearted, sunny natured boy but it did not cower him. He developed his own brilliant style of golf and in adopting the way of the Tiger showed a wonderful independence.

Then, there was the golfing world in which he was placed. Over the decade, there were many times when the rigid demarcation of amateur and professional placed barriers in Harry's golfing path. Whether it was offers to become a professional in the United States or in Australia, Harry was confronted with difficult choices. Committed to being an amateur golfer at a time when amateurism was increasingly challenged as the only meaning that could be given to the Australian golfer, Harry remained an amateur golfer. He may have been the best golfer in Australia and the best left-handed golfer in the world but when the AGU selected the amateur team to represent Australia in 1937, he found he was not the fittest.

As a young golfer of comfortable means, Harry set out to make his way in a sporting culture which offset the individualism of the sport by encouraging its members to develop a camaraderie, a sense of mateship, through sharing a social life based on the clubhouse. For most, this posed few problems. For Harry, however, gambling depleted his financial resources and drinking, his health. Yet, as the evidence mounted that, for Harry, alcohol was a disease, he consistently set himself the enormous task of pulling himself out of bad periods to return to playing top golf and to playing with dazzling form.

Timing was always an issue for Harry. The death of his father in 1933 at the young age of thirty-nine placed the family finances in the hands of two inexperienced people, his mother and himself. The appearance of Gene Sarazen in 1936 when Harry was satisfied with his amateur status and before Doll had remarried. The constant talk of an amateur team for Britain from the early 1930s that did not eventuate until 1938 when Harry's behaviour was stamped as irretrievable. The outbreak of war in 1939 when Norman Von Nida's influence on the golfing scene and on Harry was gathering momentum.

The Second World War broke the regular demands of playing top golf but not the other routines of Harry's life. As he had learned to negotiate an independent line in his childhood between the different demands of his parents, so Harry pursued his own path in a Melbourne that was changing dramatically. By now, to return to competitive golf was to go back to a world that had gone and a past he could no longer financially afford or physically accept. He accommodated himself to the present as he could. By 1961, that accommodation was broken.

* * * *

In the decade of the thirties, the golf that Harry Williams played was extraordinary. Those who watched him felt they were privileged to have witnessed him play. Even now, over sixty years on, the triumph of his easy swing, the audacity of his shots leaps off the yellowing pages of the newspaper reports. It is, as it was then, by his magnificent golf, that Harry Williams deserves his legendary status.

NOTES

Generally, references have been placed in the text but each chapter draws on material collected from a wider range of sources which is not specifically documented. The interviews were particularly important - Eileen Grigg on Harry and Doll's social world, Darryl Cox, Max Eise, Clive Glasson and Norman Von Nida on the golfing scene, Alf (Okey) King Snr, Dorothy Collins and Ray Jones on Melbourne life. The use of italicised text indicates where the narrative utilises either memories or text from the newspapers.

Chapter 1

Coroner's Report, February 1962, Public Records Office, Melbourne. Stories about Harry come from many sources for most books on Australian golf refer to him, see for instance, general histories such as Terry Smith, *Australian Golf, the first hundred years,* Lester-Townsend Publishing, 1982; Phil Tresidder, *Phil Tresidder's great days of Australian golf,* Ironbark Press, 1990 or specific club histories such as Joseph Johnson, *The Royal Melbourne Golf Club: a centenary history*, Royal Melbourne GC, c1991.

Many articles have appeared in the press relating the story of Harry Williams and anecdotes of his life: Dave Andersen, *Sporting Globe* 16 December 1961, Peter Hargraves *Sydney Sun* 8 January 1980, *Herald* 13 November 1984, Greg Hobbs *Herald* 4 January 1986, Greg Hobbs *Weekend Herald* 4-5 January 1986, *Herald* 16 January 1986, John Rice, *Sporting Globe* 14 February 1986, Tom Ramsey *Australian* 12 March 1988.

Chapter 2

For tracing the Williams family see birth, marriage and death records and electoral rolls at the State Library of Victoria and Sands and McDougall Directories were also used. For the Halfey family see Dorothy Rogers, *History of Kew,* Lowden Publishing 1973 and the entry on Halfey in the *Australian Dictionary of Biography*.

Chapters 3 and 4

Melbourne between the wars has been richly documented in a number of biographies, autobiographies and novels. Amongst the many are Keith Dunstan, *No Brains At All*, *an autobiography*, Penguin, 1990; George Johnston, *My Brother Jack*, Collins, 1964; Graham McInnes, *The Road to Gundagai*, Hamish Hamilton, 1965; Hal Porter, *The Paper Chase*, University Queensland Press, 1980; Glen Tomasetti, *Thoroughly Decent People*: *a folktale*, McPhee Gribble, 1976. For Harry's schooldays, H.L. Hall, H. Zachariah, G.F. James, *Meliora Sequamur Brighton Grammar School 1882-1982*, Brighton Grammar School, 1983. Probate records, Public Record Office, Melbourne for details of wills and estates.

Chapter 5

Jack Pollard, *Australian Golf: The Game and the Players*, Angus & Robertson, 1990 offers an encyclopaedia of information on the sport. Golf clubs and associations have commissioned histories that also provide a valuable account of the development of golf in Australia. See for instance, A. D. Ellis, *The History of the Royal Melbourne Golf Club*, vol.1, Robertson & Mullens Ltd, 1941; Gary Mansfield, *A History of Golf in Victoria*, VGA, 1987; Stewart Williams, *The test of time: the history of the Kingston Heath Golf Club*, Macmillan, 1981; Joseph Johnson's series, *The Royal Melbourne Golf Club: a centenary history*, *Birdies and billabongs: a history of the Kew Golf Club*, Kew

GC, 1994, *From Eyrie to eagles: the history of Yarra Yarra Golf Club*, Yarra Yarra GC, 1998; Don Lawrence, *Victoria Golf Club*, Lester-Townsend Publishing, 1998; John Arnold and Joseph Johnson, *Riversdale Golf Club: a centenary history*, Riversdale GC, 1982.

Horace G. Hutchinson, *Golf,* Longmans, Green & Co, 1890 and Daniel Soutar, *The Australian Golfer*, Angus & Robertson, 1906 are two classics that show the influential ideas about the sport at the turn of the century. Bernard Darwin, *Golf between the two wars*, Chatto and Windus, 1944 and C.G. Mortimer and F. Pignon, *The Story of the Open Golf championship 1860-1950*, Harrolds Publishers, 1952 were used for developments in international golf during the period.

Chapters 6 to 18

Golf columns appeared in all the major newspapers and each national championship was covered in all states. Harry's career has been traced through these sources: *Advertiser, Age, Argus, Australasian, Daily Telegraph, Herald, Leader, Referee, Smith's Weekly, Sun News Pictorial, Sydney Mail, Sydney Morning Herald, Table Talk.* As well, a succession of periodicals that have been referred to under the generic title, *Golf* included: *Golf: A Monthly Journal* 1922-32,*Tennis and Golf in Australia*, 1930-32, *Australian Golf and Tennis Magazine*, 1932-37, *Golf: Australian Golf and Tennis Magazine*, 1937-39. Two scrapbooks compiled by Harry Williams and his mother are held at Victoria Golf Club.

Throughout the narrative, Pollard's *Australian Golf* and Lawrence's *Victoria Golf Club* have been used for material on golf in Australia and at Victoria Golf Club during the decades of Harry's career. Also, David Worley, *Bill Edgar*, David Worley, 1995 offers another portrait of one of Harry's contemporaries. For New South Wales, see David J. Innes, *The Story of Golf in New South Wales 1851-1987*, NSWGA, 1988. And in Adelaide, Michael Cudmore, The Royal Adelaide Golf Club,1892-1992, Royal Adelaide G.C., 1992.

For specific topics such as the 1934 Victorian Centenary, the Minutes of the Centenary Celebrations Council were used and probate records at the Public Records Office, Melbourne for details of estates.

188

Chapter 19

For background on the post-war period, see Stella Lees and June Senyard, *The 1950s... How Australia became a modern society and everyone got a house and car*, Hyland House, 1987.

Epilogue

Russel Ward, *The Australian Legend*, 1957 and F. Scott Fitzgerald, *The Crack-Up*, Esquire, Inc., 1934 and 1936 provide fascinating insights, the former as a commentary on the construction of Harry as an Australian sporting figure and the latter for its parallels to Harry's life.

Index

88, 89, 91, 92, 93, 97, 111, 117,
121, 122, 123, 129, 138, 147,
149, 166

S

Sarazen, Gene
    4, 100, 103, 104, 126, 127, 128,
    129, 132, 133, 134, 150, 163
Sarazen, Mary 130
Sargood, Sir Frederick 37
Schlapp, Henry 61
Scott, Michael 39, 102
Shute, Densmere 104
Sinclair, Harry 64
Smith, Charlie 61, 73
Smith, Willie 163
Soutar, Daniel 33, 64
Spence, Arthur 37
Stegley, Brian 152, 175
Stewart, Rufus 87, 147

T

Tanner, Tom 142, 147
Taylor, H. J. 44, 76
Theodore, Ted 60
Thompson, Don 97, 106
Thompson, George 78
Thomson, Hector 119
Thomson, Jimmy 104
Thomson, Peter 176
Titus, Jack (Skinny) 113
Tolhurst, Susie 57
Trumble, J. W. 102

U

Uren, Bill 42

V

Vicars, Sir John 77
Von Nida, Norman
    4, 131, 132, 140, 147, 162, 168,
    169, 170, 171, 172, 176

W

Waler, J. 147
Walker, Captain 79
Walker, Don 159
Walker, Joyce 159
Waterson, Alan 167
Weir, Bob 161
Welch, Eric 156
Whitton, Ivo
    4, 39, 47, 56, 57, 61, 66, 73, 74,
    77, 88, 91, 97, 121, 123, 143,
    144, 148
Williams, Joan Dagmar
    14, 17, 19, 20, 30
Williams, Mary 6
Wilson, Ray 155
Winser, Legh 87, 162
Wishart, Bill 149
Wood, Craig 104
Worley, David 57

Y

Young, Jock 140, 141
Young, John 83

Z

Zaharias, George 165